BLAKE LIVELY
Traveling to the Top!

BLAKE LIVELY
Traveling to the Top!

By Emily Robin

SCHOLASTIC INC.

New York   Toronto   London   Auckland   Sydney
Mexico City   New Delhi   Hong Kong   Buenos Aires

Front cover photo:
Michael Loccisano/Film Magic/Getty Images
Back cover photo: Brad Barket/Getty Images
Poster
Front:
Rob Loud/Getty Images
Back:
Clockwise from top left:
DiSciullo/bauergriffinonline.com
Scott Gries/Getty Images
Larry Busacca/WireImage/Getty Images
James Devaney/WireImage/Getty Images
Steve Sands/bauergriffinonline.com
Steve Sands/bauergriffinonline.com
Mark Sullivan/WireImage/Getty Images

ISBN-13: 978-0-545-13916-8
ISBN-10: 0-545-13916-3

12 11 10 9 8 7 6 5 4 3 2 1   9 10 11 12 13 14/0

Cover and interior designed by Deena Fleming
Printed in the U.S.A.
First printing, February 2009

Table of Contents

BLAKE LIVELY
Traveling to the Top!

Introduction

I t was a typically sunny day in California in 2004. A casting panel for a new film, including the casting director, producers, and director, had been watching auditions all day long for a role in their teen movie based on the *New York Times* bestselling book *The Sisterhood of the Traveling Pants*. Three major stars had already snatched up three of the main roles, and there was just one girl left to cast. The role of "Bridget" called for a young, fresh-faced actress with a strong look and a big presence on screen. They needed someone special to play the sporty, no-nonsense leader of the four girls — someone who looked like she could work hard and play hard. Multiple actresses had gone out for the role, but none of them had really wowed the panel. All of that changed when a young actress with no experience walked in and read for the role.

Blake Lively, a teenager from a well-known Hollywood family, came in and handed the agents her headshot. They flipped it over, expecting a résumé, but the back of her photo was blank. At first they thought the teen was kidding. No one comes to an audition without a résumé, even if it is short! But Blake wasn't joking. She had little experience outside of a tiny role in a film that was never released, and a few acting classes. She was really only auditioning to make her older brother Eric happy. He and the rest of Blake's family had been involved in show business for years, however Blake had never been interested in joining them. But Eric encouraged her to give acting a shot before dismissing it altogether. This was only Blake's third audition for her brother's agent, and so far she wasn't all that impressed with the auditioning process. But she was determined to give it a fair shot for Eric's sake.

So, after waiting for everyone in the room to get over her lack of a résumé, Blake took her mark and began to read her lines. After watching her go through a few scenes, the panel was absolutely shocked. This inexperienced, largely untrained sixteen-year-old was exactly what they had been looking for. She got right down to the core of the character immediately, and expertly captured the vulnerability mixed with toughness that defined "Bridget" in the panel's minds. After Blake thanked them for the opportunity and left the room, the group erupted in conversation. They were in awe of Blake's talent and they knew, without a doubt, that she was the only actress they wanted for the role. They could easily see what Blake hadn't seen in herself yet — that she had the charisma and natural stage presence to become a huge star.

A few days later, Eric's agent called her with the good news — she had been offered the role of "Bridget" in *The Sisterhood of the Traveling Pants*. Blake was psyched to land the role, but she still just thought of it as something to do over the summer before finishing up high school and heading to college. However, once she walked on to the set and began filming, Blake fell in love with acting. Suddenly, acting was vying with college as a possibility for the near future. But Blake still wasn't convinced that acting was the way to go . . . at least she wasn't until *The Sisterhood of the Traveling Pants* hit theaters.

When the film premiered to millions of fans and glowing reviews, Blake couldn't possibly have been prepared for that response! She absolutely loved it and, after that, there was no way she could go back to a life without acting. She never would have guessed then that she would go on to become a mega star with millions of fans, that young girls would copy her look, or that the media would begin to watch her every move. All she knew was that she loved entertaining people. She loved the rush of seeing fans react to her work and she loved the thrill of knowing that she had inspired people. So, despite her reservations, Blake closed her eyes, took a deep breath, and jumped headfirst into stardom.

Chapter 1: The Littlest Lively

The Lively family received quite the surprise on a warm, late summer day on August 25, 1987. The whole family was gathered at a hospital in Tarzana, California, waiting to meet the newest addition to the Lively clan — a baby boy they had been expecting for nine months. Elaine and Ernie Lively had already picked out a name for their new son — Blake. But the littlest Lively defied expectations from the very beginning. Instead of an adorable boy, the baby turned out to be a beautiful, blue-eyed girl. The family was incredibly excited, but they weren't at all prepared for her. "Actually, my grandma's brother's name was Blake, and my sister wrote it down when she was reading a family tree," the actress revealed. "And they said, 'If it's a boy, we'll name him Blake, and if it's a girl, we'll name her Blakely.' And everybody thought I was going to be a boy, and then I came out and I was a girl. And they had already been calling me Blake for months because they were positive I was going to be a boy. And they had been calling me Blake for so long, they just [kept it]," as Blake told *Radio Free Entertainment*. So the name stuck, and the newest Lively became Blake Christina Lively.

The Lively clan is a large and loving family, and Blake's never once doubted how lucky she is to have them, as she explained in the August 2008 issue of *Seventeen* magazine. "When I care about somebody, whether it's my best friend or somebody who I would date, I give them all of my heart. I've just been so loved, and I'm used to really loving people and trusting them." Her parents, Ernie and Elaine Lively, have been happily married since December 1979, and are currently living in Tarzana, California. Elaine has three children from a previous marriage, Jason, Lori, and Robyn. They are all extremely close to their stepfather, and Ernie considers them to be his children, too. Ernie and Elaine also have a son named Eric who was born five years before Blake. Blake's older siblings were ecstatic to welcome her into the family, especially since she was such an adorable and happy child. No one could get enough of little Blake's grin and infectious laugh. It certainly didn't take long before she had everyone wrapped around her little finger.

Acting was in Blake's blood from the very beginning. Her father is a popular character actor who has appeared in over one hundred different television shows, including *The Dukes of Hazzard*; *Quantum Leap*; *The X-Files*; *Murder, She Wrote*; *Malibu Shores*; and *The West Wing*. He also ran acting classes and coached a number of rising stars in Hollywood in the 1980's and 1990's, like Brittany Murphy, Kristy Swanson, Alyson Hannigan, and Jason Priestley. Blake's mother is an acting coach and manager, and even did a little acting and modeling herself when she was younger. As she explained to *New York* magazine: "In my day I modeled under the name Willie Elaine Lively. After having three babies, I posed in Jantzen swimsuits for *Harper's Bazaar* and *Glamour*." No wonder Blake is so beautiful and talented, she got some pretty good genes from her mom and dad!

And it isn't just Blake's parents who are talented — her siblings are all show business veterans, too. Blake's brother Eric has modeled for the trendy clothing brand Abercrombie & Fitch, and has had starring roles on television shows including *So Weird*, *The L Word*, and *Modern Men*. Blake's half-brother Jason starred as Rusty Griswold in 1985's *National Lampoon's European Vacation*. Half-sister Lori is a character actress like her stepfather, Ernie.

She has been in numerous television shows, including *Star Trek: Deep Space Nine*, *Melrose Place*, er, *Cold Case*, and *Two and a Half Men*. And, last, but not least, half-sister Robyn inspired underappreciated girls everywhere to take control of their destinies with her starring role as Louise in 1989's *Teen Witch*. In addition, she's been acting since she was little, appearing in shows like *Punky Brewster* and *21 Jump Street*. She went on to star in shows like *Twin Peaks*, *Chicago Hope*, and *Savannah*. Blake's half-siblings are all significantly older than she is—Jason was eighteen when Blake was born and Robyn was fifteen—so they were already pretty famous by the time Blake came into the world. Which means that Blake grew up living with fame, since fans often recognized her well-known brothers and sisters.

With everyone in the family working in show business, Blake spent a lot of time hanging out on movie sets. In fact, Blake saw a set before she ever even saw her own home, as she told *Radio Free Entertainment*: "The day I was born, when I came home from the hospital, I literally didn't go to my house. I went to my sister's set." As she explained to the *Boston Herald*, growing up with her family involved in show business has really helped her with her own career. "I think it's great that they're [her family] all in it . . . They're very helpful and understanding." Blake had a great time going to work with her parents and siblings when she was little. It must have been very cool playing in the wardrobe department, running around movie studios' incredible sets, and getting a behind-the-scenes look at how movies and television shows are made. Directors and producers loved having Blake on set. The cheerful toddler was easygoing, well-behaved, and absolutely adorable! With her blonde corkscrew curls, big blue eyes, and freckles she charmed everyone she met. She was so at home on sets that Blake's parents thought she might want to try acting herself. So Blake made a couple of forays into the industry when she was little, but none of those experiences made her want to pursue a career in the family business.

When Blake was five, her parents heard that producers were looking for a young actress to play Robin Williams's daughter in a comedy called *Mrs. Doubtfire* that would premiere in 1993. In the film, the always-hilarious actor would be playing Daniel Hillard, a father who only gets to see his kids once a week because of his divorce. So, in order to spend more time with his children, Hillard dresses up as an older woman named Mrs. Doubtfire and applies to be their new nanny. Daniel's ex-wife hires him, and hilarity ensues as Daniel tries to keep his ex and children from discovering that he is the new nanny. In the end, Daniel is exposed, but his behavior proves how much he loves his kids, and his nanny skills impress his wife enough that he is allowed to spend more time with his children.

Blake's parents encouraged her to audition for *Mrs. Doubtfire*, and she thought it might be fun, so she went out for the role of Robin Williams's youngest daughter, "Natalie." Blake made it through the first few rounds of auditions easily, and soon she was one of two finalists for the role. Blake was up against Mara Wilson, an already accomplished child actress. Both girls had to audition with Robin himself. Blake was terrified! Robin Williams has long been regarded as one of the funniest comics of all time, and he was a huge star! To calm her nerves, Blake's parents told her that she would be auditioning with Robin's twin brother instead of the actor himself. Blake believed them and delivered an impressive audition, but, in the end, Mara won the role. Mara was very talented, and she looked more like Robin and Sally Field, who was playing Robin's ex-wife. Blake was probably pretty disappointed that she didn't get the part, even though she knew what a good actress Mara was. The whole process had been exciting, but scary and ultimately disappointing. Blake loved being around movies and television shows, but she just wasn't sure it was what she wanted for herself. In fact, Blake didn't even think about acting again until she was ten years old. In 1998, Blake's father produced a little movie called *Sandman*. Ernie also directed the film, and he cast Blake, Eric, and Lori in small roles. Blake played "Trixie" and the "Tooth Fairy," while her brother and sister played "Bobby" and "Kim Doll."

Sandman took place in the fictional Fantasyworld. There, Early Knapp, whose job it is to help children sleep, decides to retire. He feels like children no longer believe in him or believe that they need to sleep. But his boss won't let him quit. She takes him out into the world to investigate. They meet a child named Tina who can see Early and his boss and she ends up stealing their magic. She uses the magic to free all of the world's children from nightly sleep. Early and his boss must then rally all of the citizens of Fantasyworld to convince children to go to sleep again. Eventually the kids see how important sleep is, Early goes back to work, and balance is restored.

For Blake, being in a movie wasn't that much different than hanging out on her family's sets. She was used to the hustle and bustle of filming, the food from craft services, and the long days. The only difference on the *Sandman* set was that Blake performed in a few scenes. Going through hair and makeup, wardrobe, and memorizing lines was a new and exciting process for Blake. It was a lot of work for someone who was used to playing on sets, but it was a fun challenge, too. And there was still plenty of time for goofing around. Blake and the rest of the cast had a great time hanging out together between takes, especially on the elaborate and fantastical sets. But, her favorite part of that film by far was spending time with her older brother and sister. Since Lori was significantly older than Blake and Eric, she didn't always get to spend as much time with them as she would have liked. And Blake and Eric loved the quality time with their big sister!

The Lively family was very proud of the finished film, but unfortunately, Ernie was never able to acquire a distributor for the film so *Sandman* was never released. Everyone who worked on the film was disappointed, but the whole process was a good experience for the Livelys. It was especially helpful for Blake, since it gave her an idea of what being an actress was like, instead of just watching her family members perform. Blake did a wonderful job playing both of her parts. She was adorable as Trixie and enchanting as the Tooth Fairy, and her family and the rest of the cast and crew were all impressed with her talent and professionalism. But Blake wasn't wowed by the whole experience. "I've grown up on sets — my mom is a manager and always has kids come in for coaching, my family's always going over lines for an audition, I'm always stealing craft service. So it was so much a part of my life that I never felt a desire for it. And it seemed like such a nightmare. That [was] the last thing in the world I want to do," Blake told *Radio Free Entertainment*. Acting in her dad's film had been fun, but Blake had a lot of other interests and she didn't necessarily want to be just like everyone else in her family. "My whole family's in the business," Lively explained on *Today* in 2005. "I never really went after it, just because it was already so much a part of my life." Always-unique Blake was more interested in forging her own path.

So instead of focusing on a career in show business, Blake decided to follow different interests and dreams. She tried any activity that caught her eye, focused on her education, and just generally enjoyed being a kid!

Chapter 2: Sweet School Girl

Considering that Blake's life was immersed in Hollywood culture from the very beginning, her childhood was actually surprisingly normal. Yes, she spent a lot of time on movie and television sets, and fans recognized her brothers, sisters, and father fairly often, but none of that seemed strange to Blake. In fact, Blake loved doing all of the same things that her friends did, and unless someone knew she came from a show business family, they never would have guessed from talking to her! Blake was an extremely curious child, and she loved trying new things. Her happy-go-lucky attitude and willingness to try just about anything made her a blast to spend time with. She played every imaginable sport, baked cookies while doing her homework, spent days at the beach, and had sleepovers with the other girls on her street.

Blake's friends thought she was silly and goofy, and they respected her because she was never afraid to make a fool of herself in the name of having fun or taking one for the team. Blake loved playing sports and she was a great player to have around because she followed directions well and gave everything she tried 110 percent. Coaches loved having Blake on their teams, even if she wasn't the best player, as Blake recounted to *Radio Free Entertainment*: "I played soccer when I was little for about three years. And I wasn't very good at it, but I was always much taller than the rest of the kids, so they always had me on the defensive line. They would never let me kick the ball around, because I guess I wasn't very good at that. I was just like tall, lanky, and clumsy. But when you're little, everybody crowds around the ball. You don't stay in your positions. Everybody just goes for it. And so they would always say to me, 'Make sure you stay in your position.' And then when everybody would get clumped around the ball, they would say, 'Blake!' And my job was just to go barreling through the crowd so that the kids ran away because this large beast is charging at them. And then the ball would be free for the good player to get the ball and kick it down the field." Soccer didn't turn out to be the best fit for Blake, but she did excel at things like dance and drama, where she could really perform.

In school, Blake was a natural achiever. She excelled at every subject and wowed her teachers with her strong work ethic. Blake also got along with other students easily, which was a great skill to have, especially since Blake switched schools often. She would eventually attend thirteen schools, as well as being home-schooled. She also took acting classes taught by her mother and father with other young actors and actress like her future *Gossip Girl* co-star Penn Badgley (but more on him later!). Blake really enjoyed home-schooling, because she was able to move forward at her own pace and focus on the subjects that interested her. But home-schooling was ultimately not the right fit for Blake. She loved the social aspect of school and missed joining clubs, giggling with her friends at lunch, and passing notes during classes. Plus, having other students around helped motivate Blake to push herself to even greater academic achievements.

When Blake reached ninth grade, she began attending Burbank High School. She got to stay there for all of high school, and she loved it! After switching schools so many times in the past, Blake made sure to take advantage of every moment there. She had no problem fitting in and soon had tons of friends. She got very involved in school activities, and quickly became known for her enthusiasm. Blake was probably the most spirited student Burbank High had ever seen. She was a varsity cheerleader and she loved dressing up in school colors, going to watch football and basketball games, and working on decorations for school dances. "I was really involved in my school…[I was] the only person to dress up on Spirit Days. No one had spirit, so I made up for everyone. I miss school. I actually miss writing essays!" Blake told CosmoGirl.com. Blake even dressed up as Burbank's mascot, a bulldog, for pep rallies! She loved putting on that big costume and hamming it up in front of the crowd to get everyone pumped up for games. Even then, performing came easily for Blake!

Blake was extremely involved at her high school. She joined six different clubs, worked on fund-raisers and charity projects, joined Burbank's nationally recognized show choir, and even became her class's president. "I'm happy to say that I tried every sport and activity in high school, or just growing up. So that was fun. I had a wonderful time. I think it makes your school experience and memories just so much better. I would always go over to talk to people and I would try to get them involved. I sound ridiculous, but I would try to get them involved in activities. Because there's an activity for everyone, even if you don't think it's for you. Like I can't sing or dance to save my life, and I was in the number one show choir in the nation—all you do is sing and dance. And I was always, like, front and center singing as loud as I could, because I loved it. I was so passionate about it. And the people that I met in this group were so fantastic. So I think that if you get involved, you have this wonderful group of people that you have a class with during the day, you spend extracurricular time with—they become your friends, they become like your family, and you share this love of an activity or a sport. I think it's really, really important for kids to get involved in school. I just think everybody would be a lot happier. I sound really silly, but it's true," Blake told *Radio Free Entertainment*.

Blake's spirit and willingness to try new things and get involved earned her the respect of classmates. She was a real leader within her high school, as class president, and as a role model for other students. Blake was wholesome, funny, and fun to hang out with. She didn't need to party or use drugs or alcohol to connect with her peers. "I had a lot of friends in high school, but I was never the wild party girl. Never have been, never plan to be!" Blake explained to *InStyle* magazine. Blake was popular because she was able to connect with people about the important things in life, and she ended up with a great group of friends. "Burbank feels like a small *town* in the big city of L.A. So for a fun night out, we would go to school fund-raisers. I was very involved in school — I was class president! And all of my friends were good — nobody was too wild.... But I think at the core, everyone deals with similar things in high school: jealousy, people making up rumors, dating someone you shouldn't, or wanting to be with someone who's unattainable," Blake dished to *Seventeen* magazine.

High school was also special for Blake because she got her first real taste of romance during that time. At the beginning of her senior year, Blake began dating her first boyfriend, actor Kelly Blatz, a cutie she's known for years. "I've had a crush on him since second grade," Blake told the *Boston Herald* in 2005. "He finally came around this year." Once the two started dating, they were pretty insep-arable, and Kelly made Blake very happy. Since Kelly and Blake had known each other since they were little, they already had an incredible friendship that they built their relationship on. Blake has never been one to jump into romance quickly, and her relationship with Kelly was no exception. The two slowly progressed from being friends, to dating, to being exclusive. Kelly supported Blake through a senior year full of big choices about college and her future. He was very proud of his beautiful, accomplished, talented girlfriend and, although they've since broken up, Blake and Kelly are still friends.

Blake had an amazing high school experience. She would probably encourage all of her fans to cherish their time in high school, and not to be afraid to get involved and meet lots of different types of people. "Being involved gives you a purpose. It gives you a reason to go to school every day. So I think you have to go and do it — no inhibitions. If you go into things unsure of yourself, it can be taken as being snooty or not being nice, and people will shut you down for that. You have to be willing to take a plunge now and then, because it's worth it. It's all about taking a risk," Blake explained in *Seventeen* magazine. Getting involved in a variety of clubs helped Blake make lots of different types of friends. Stepping outside of her comfort zone and becoming friends with people she wouldn't have met otherwise turned out to be one of the best parts about high school for Blake, and she would want her fans to try it too. As she told *Seventeen* magazine, "I had a really big group of friends. And I know it sounds really cheesy, but I was in like six different clubs, and each had different groups of people. And we were nothing alike, but we all had this common passion—so it was really a great bonding experience." So, to follow Blake's example, try getting involved in a new club at school or volunteer to help decorate for the school dance, even if your regular friends aren't into it. You might meet some really cool new friends—or even a cute boy!

Blake loved being in school so much that she probably would have been happy if high school had lasted even longer than four years. But Blake was looking forward to four more years of education at Stanford University. She couldn't wait to move into a dorm, meet her roommate, stay up late studying in the library, and trying out a variety of interesting classes. College was the only option Blake could see for her future, until something happened her sophomore year that would change her life forever.

Chapter 3: The Right Fit

When Blake was in tenth grade, she and her older brother went on a very memorable trip that changed Blake's entire perspective on life and set her on track for her current career. "My brother Eric [he's the best brother in the world, he's my closest sibling in age], in the middle of my sophomore year, decided that I needed to be more cultured and took me around Europe for two months, while I was taking world history. And we went everywhere—London, Cambridge, Florence, Venice, Rome, Cologne, Brussels, Paris. So he's been amazing. He's been like a third parent to me. And he sat me down when we were in Europe and said, 'What are you going to do with your life?' I'm fifteen at the time. And so he made like a chart of things I could possibly do, and nothing really interested me. And then like a year later, he said, 'I think you're going to be an actress.' He [told] his agents, 'You have to start sending Blake out on auditions.' And I didn't want to make him mad because he's such a good brother, so I just went on auditions to appease him," Blake explained to *Radio Free Entertainment*. Blake was very hesitant at first to even try acting at all, as she told the Associated Press, "I had no clue what I wanted to do, but I knew it was not acting—just because my whole family was in it, and it was the only job I really knew of. And I thought, 'That's really cool but that's not something I want to do.'" But Blake went on the auditions that Eric set up for her, because she's never been one to dismiss something without giving it a fair shot. She wasn't particularly prepared to be thrust into the cutthroat world of auditions in Hollywood, as all she had to take with her was a photo of herself, a good attitude, and a willingness to try something new.

Then on her third audition, Blake went out for a part in the film adaptation of the popular book series *The Sisterhood of the Traveling Pants*. The books are about four best friends who find a pair of seemingly magical jeans that fit all four of them perfectly, even though they are all very different shapes and sizes. The girls are Bridget, the sporty leader; Tibby, the artsy rebel; Carmen, the Latina drama queen; and Lena, the shy artist. Each summer, these lifelong friends are split up as they go off on their own adventures, but they mail the pants back and forth to each other as a way to stay connected. The film's focus was on the incredible friendship the girls have, and how that friendship provides them with the strength they need to face life's most difficult challenges. In the movie, Bridget goes to soccer camp in Mexico, Lena goes to Greece to visit her grandparents, Carmen heads to the South to spend time with her father, and Tibby stays in their hometown to make a documentary while working at a local drugstore. Each girl faces some difficult situations—Bridget has a disappointing first romantic experience, Tibby meets a little girl losing a battle to cancer, Lena falls in love with a boy her grandparents don't approve of, and Carmen faces her father getting remarried. However, in the end, the girls help each other work through their problems and pain, and triumph in the end.

Any of the main roles in *Sisterhood of the Traveling Pants* would be a dream come true for a young actress. The parts had depth, and the roles were dynamic and challenging—plus the movie was sure to resonate with and inspire other young girls. Blake was certainly aware of that when she auditioned. She knew that if she was going to become an actress, she wanted to take parts with real substance, and the role of Bridget certainly had it! The roles of Lena, Tibby, and Carmen had already been cast when Blake auditioned. But by the time Blake walked out of that audition, everyone knew that she was the only choice to play Bridget Vreeland. Blake was extremely excited when she got the news. She might not have planned to go into acting, but once she had gotten such a great role, she was going to give it everything she had.

Blake was probably pretty nervous to film her first big movie, especially since her castmates were already big stars in their own rights. America Ferrera, already a favorite of critics for her role in *Real Women Have Curves*, played sassy Carmen. Amber Tamblyn, star of the television show *Joan of Arcadia*, was all set to play angst-ridden Tibby. And Alexis Bledel, star of the wildly popular CW show *Gilmore Girls*, was on board to play soulful Lena. Each of Blake's co-stars were experienced professionals—and none of them were teenagers! Blake, at age sixteen, was, by far, the youngest of the stars. Luckily, Blake wasn't completely alone. Her father, Ernie, had been cast as Bridget's father in the film, so Blake had a little piece of home along with her on set! Whenever Blake felt overwhelmed by her starring role or was nervous before filming a crucial scene, Dad was there to give Blake a pep talk and remind her how much he and the rest of her family believed in her. He was incredibly proud of his youngest child and her first real foray into the business he'd loved for so many years.

As it turned out, Blake had no reason to be nervous about being the youngest or the least experienced. She clicked with her castmates right away and the girls became very close very fast.

"We became incredibly good friends when we were up there [in Vancouver]. Really, really close friends, fast, which is interesting because that's what it needed for the movie. But it just happened to be that it worked that way. Usually, you get girls with like minds and it just happens, I guess," Amber Tamblyn told About.com. "We were inseparable. Like, whenever we did our scenes together, we had sleepovers at America's and just everything, like we went out to dinner with each other. I'd go jogging with America in the morning, we'd work out together, we'd go hiking together, we'd eat dinner, breakfast, lunch together. Go see movies."

All of that bonding certainly showed when the girls began filming, as they had real chemistry together on screen. It was much easier to act like they liked and respected each other since they really did! "Alexis, America, and Amber and I formed a really good friendship on the first *Sisterhood* movie. I mean, I was in high school at the time, and a lot of times girls are insecure and aren't so nice to one another. So it was really refreshing to have three females who could help one another, who were happy for each other, and love each other," Blake explained in *Seventeen* magazine. Blake was also able to draw upon her friendships from back home to help portray the depth of feeling and loyalty she needed to feel as Bridget, as she explained to About.com: "I have a friend, my friend Jessica, who I've had since I was three years old and my friend Brittany who I've had since... seventh grade. We can fight like no tomorrow and we can have these crazy times and prank, and go do nothing together and it's this great friendship because you have such a deep understanding of one another. We know each other so well inside and out that it's amazing." Going through the filming process only intensified the newly minted friendship of the four girls, and it's still going strong today!

After the girls were finished filming their scenes together, they split up and headed out to the locations where they would film their separate stories. Blake flew down to Mexico to film her scenes at the beach, which certainly wasn't a bad spot to spend the summer! Blake's character Bridget is the sporty, aggressive leader of the friends. She is a real go-getter who works hard and plays hard, but she struggles emotionally with her unresolved feelings about her mother. Bridget's mother suffered from depression and committed suicide, and Bridget has worked very hard to be happy and live her life to the fullest to try to prove she isn't like her mother. This leads misguided Bridget to pursue a relationship she isn't ready for with one of the slightly older soccer coaches at her summer camp. The relationship really hurts Bridget emotionally, and leaves her feeling empty and alone. But as soon as her friends learn what happened, they hurry to her side and help her work through it when she returns from camp.

The scenes in Mexico were very physically challenging for Blake. She had to play a lot of soccer, and she had to look like a very accomplished athlete while doing it. While Blake had played soccer, she had never been very good at it. So making Bridget look like a star wasn't easy for Blake. Luckily, Blake loves a challenge as much as her character, Bridget, so she was psyched to get back into soccer. "I had two months of soccer training through trainers in Los Angeles and Canada. My brother-in-law took me to all the games with him and his friends, and I played with the other girls in Canada. I played for three years when I was young and I was absolutely horrible at it, but I loved it. So, when they told me I'd have to learn how to play soccer I was so excited because it's such a fun sport to play," Blake told About.com. In the end, Blake's hard work paid off, because she really looked like a soccer powerhouse in the film!

In addition to all of the sports action, Blake had another challenge to cope with—her first on-screen romance scenes. Hunky Mike Vogel played "Eric," Bridget's love interest in the film. With his sandy blond hair and adorable grin, Mike was pretty irresistible, so Blake was probably pretty nervous to kiss him, especially with the crew and her father watching from off screen. But Mike was really good at putting Blake at ease. They developed a great friendship, and Mike spent a lot of time teasing his co-star about her youth and her love of Britney Spears's music. So when the time came, their kissing scenes were actually less romantic and nerve-wracking than Blake had expected them to be. It was her first on-screen kiss, but with so many people watching, cameras in their faces, and a boom mike looming overhead, it was definitely more work than play to kiss the cutie. In the end though, Mike and Blake's chemistry made their attraction completely believable on the big screen, and Blake's friends were definitely jealous that she got such an adorable love interest!

Blake had had such an unforgettable time working on her first movie that she was very sad when filming ended. She had never wanted to be an actress, but she had loved every second of working on *Sisterhood* and was very proud of what she had accomplished. To promote the film, she and her castmates were sent across the country to do interviews and publicity events. They didn't get to do the interviews together, so Blake was on her own! It was Blake's first real taste of all of the work that goes into promoting a movie, and she had a great time doing it. "I went on a press tour for *Sisterhood*, which I thought, 'I get to see all these great cities!' And it's from like five in the morning till ten o'clock at night, you're just doing interviews and radio shows, and then you get in a plane and fly to the next city. So you were like barely awake in the car, waving to the Statue of Liberty.... But it was so much fun!" Blake told *Radio Free Entertainment*. Blake went to Philadelphia, Washington, Toronto, Denver, and New York — and her favorite was, by far, New York, as she told *Radio Free Entertainment*: "We got to have this wonderful weekend in New York where I saw *Rent* and *Wicked* ... And they said, 'You have this much per diem per day.' So I got massages and room service. I mean, it was an amazing break. The two-day weekend was the best weekend I've ever had in my life!" After that tour, Blake really realized just how much she loved being in show business, and things were only getting more exciting as she anticipated the release of the film.

When the movie premiered in theaters on June 1, 2005, Blake was probably super nervous about how fans would respond, but she had nothing to worry about. The movie was a hit, bringing in over $39 million total at the box office. Blake took her boyfriend at the time, Kelly Blatz, to the premiere, and had a blast working the red carpet. Seeing her work up on the big screen and watching as viewers reacted to the story was a very inspiring moment for Blake. The film, with its universal issues and themes, really resonated with a much wider audience than originally expected. The producers knew that young girls and women would really relate to the film, but they hadn't been expecting the interest of so many boys and men. "I think that people saw the title and they got really scared away [originally]. *The Sisterhood*, first of all, screams chick flick. *Of the Traveling Pants*? Like what does that mean? That there's magical pants dancing around at Hogwarts?

I think the title scared a lot of people away. But like ninety percent of men we talked to said that they cried during it. And they said, 'I didn't think that it was going to be a movie that I would even like, but I loved it.' Because it seemed like it would be feminine issues — you know, like 'my prom dress' or 'this boy that I have a crush on doesn't know I exist.' But it was really universal issues, and serious issues," Blake told *Radio Free Entertainment*. She couldn't believe how many people *The Sisterhood of the Traveling Pants* touched and she was very honored to have had such an impact on so many fans.

As *The Sisterhood of the Traveling Pants* continued to gain momentum at the box office, Blake became an overnight sensation. Her popularity was a little overwhelming to the young actress, and it opened a lot of doors for her. She wasn't exactly being followed by the paparazzi, but fans were recognizing her everywhere she went. Blake's agent and family encouraged her to take advantage of her success while she could, but Blake had her own ideas. "Everybody was telling me, 'Oh, you can't go back to high school. You can't finish your senior year. You gotta keep doing movies now, get yourself out there.' ... I was very involved in school: I was class president, I was in a nationally competitive show choir, I was in cheerleading, I was in all AP classes, six different clubs. So it was my life. I was at every fund-raiser, every event.... But, you know, I went back to school my senior year and decided I would take a year or so off to act. And that's what I've been doing ever since. So I love it. And here I am," Blake told the Associated Press. So, contrary to everyone's advice, Blake went back to school and had the time of her life during her senior year of high school. She took advantage of the time with her friends, remained active in all of her extracurricular activities, and enjoyed one more year of being a kid. Then, as graduation drew near, Blake made plans to pick up where she had left off after *The Sisterhood of the Traveling Pants*.

Chapter 4: Film 101

Blake had achieved the goal she had been working towards since she entered school—she had graduated from high school and been accepted to Stanford University, one of the most prestigious schools in the country. But after filming *The Sisterhood of the Traveling Pants*, Blake had begun to dream of becoming an actress. Unfortunately, it was going to be impossible for Blake to be a college freshman at Stanford while also making movies. Going to college is a full-time job and Blake wouldn't have been able to take time off for auditions and acting jobs, and still keep up with the demanding coursework at a top tier school. "Everybody that was involved in my professional career said, 'This is the time. You have to do a movie back to back to back.' Whatever. And I said, 'No, school is so important to me.' So [I compromised] and I said, 'I'll take a year off. What would be my first year of college, I'll just completely dedicate to acting,'" Blake explained to *Radio Free Entertainment*. So, with the clock ticking on her year of acting, Blake took the plunge and threw herself into becoming a star.

As luck would have it, Blake's first big role after high school was starring in a movie all about going to college. Released in 2006, *Accepted* is a goofy, sometimes gross, but ultimately very intelligent comedy. It is all about a group of kids who start their own college, The South Harmon Institute of Technology, when they don't get accepted to any of the colleges they applied to. Blake played the role of "Monica Moreland," the dream girl of "Bartleby Gaines," the main character in the film who was played by Justin Long. Monica is the beautiful, very popular girl in Bartleby's high school that he has had a crush on since sixth grade. But Monica only sees Bartleby as a friend, and she also happens to be dating an older guy, one of the meanest fraternity members at Harmon College. Monica gets in to Harmon College, which is just up the hill from Bartleby's fake school. After catching her boyfriend cheating on her and struggling with confusing course catalogs, credit requirements, and high stress classes, Monica becomes disillusioned with her college experience. Luckily, Bartleby's innovative college restores her faith in education, and Bartleby's wooing restores her faith in romance. Monica and Bartleby eventually end up dating and she transfers to his school at the end of the film.

What made *Accepted* such an interesting film to Blake is that it had a very powerful message about the American education system. Bartleby and his friends created South Harmon because they couldn't face the pressure and disappointment from their parents when they didn't get into other schools. Bartleby and his friends are smart, creative, and interesting—they just haven't conformed to the strict standards that most colleges demand of their students. But Bartleby's website is so believable that other kids think it is real and show up for orientation! Instead of rejecting the hundreds of kids who have already been rejected from every other school, Bartleby decides to try to make it work. He allows the students to make up their own classes and become their own teachers. Surprisingly, the system works. The students are allowed to express themselves freely, learn about a variety of subjects, and be creative. They learn because they want to learn, not because they are being forced to take certain classes. The school is eventually exposed as a fake and shut down, but Bartleby appeals to the Accreditation Board. There he gives a rousing speech about the failures of conventional education and convinces the board to give South Harmon a chance. The board reopens the school and everyone wins!

Blake definitely believes in getting a good education — she was all set to go to Stanford, after all — but she also understood and believed in the film's message. She had felt the pressure to get into a good college and had worked very hard to do so. But Blake had also taken time to travel and try things outside of the world of academia that she feels gave her a broader perspective about life and education. "So many times in school, you get so bogged down by things that you 'have to do' to get into a good college. And you end up being so overwhelmed that you don't do a great job at any one thing. You're just like dying and half-doing a million different activities. And activities that you're involved in, the extracurriculars you have to take, have nothing to do with real life experience. Like why, in high school, don't they teach you how to do taxes? So I think it's really important to have real life experience. It's so important to travel and just get out in the world. I think it would be great if everybody just deferred college for one year and just traveled and just experienced life, and then went away to school. I think you would know what you want to do more...So, yes, I think it's a good message," Blake told *Radio Free Entertainment*. Students across the country definitely connected with the message. The film pulled in over $36 million at the box office and was nominated for two Teen Choice Awards.

Blake herself was learning more than she ever dreamed possible during her year of acting. Working with amazing actors like Justin Long, Jonah Hill, Ann Cusack, and Lewis Black was an education in and of itself. Blake learned more about comedic timing, improvisation, and physical comedy on that set than she could ever have learned in an acting class. "It's a comedy but not your stereotypical slapstick kind. The actors were all really smart, quirky, and sarcastic. A lot of them have worked with Ben Stiller, Vince Vaughn and Steve Carell, and it was so much fun! During the entire shoot, I was cracking up!" Blake gushed to CosmoGirl.com. Filming a lot of the scenes felt more like play than work to Blake, like cheering her head off with a huge crowd while Bartleby sang on stage, or dancing as sprinklers soaked everyone in a party scene, or telling off the film's bad guy. Plus, watching Justin Long and Jonah Hill outdo each other improvising had Blake and the rest of the cast and crew in giggles almost every single day. The *Accepted* set was incredibly fun and easygoing, and Blake had a great time working on the movie.

Blake's other film of 2006 was a far cry from the light-hearted *Accepted*. It was a horror flick called *Simon Says* about a psychotic killer who terrorizes a group of college kids. However, filming *Simon Says* wasn't horrific for Blake at all since her boyfriend at the time, Kelly Blatz, her father, her two sisters, and her brother-in-law, Bart Johnson, were all in the film with her! The gory film was produced by Blake's dad and, although it was never released in the U.S., it did garner some attention at the Brussels International Festival of Fantastic Film on April 9, 2007. It was also nominated for "Most Anticipated Film" at the 2006 Spike Scream Awards. And scenes from the movie were leaked onto the Internet, where it got great responses from fans who thought the movie's bloody scenes had a nice touch of humor to them.

Simon Says told the story of a group of college students on spring break at a cursed lakeside campsite. When their friends begin disappearing, the remaining kids must try to play the game the killer has set up for them if they want to survive. The movie was very gory, but it also had some funny moments. The special effects weren't exactly realistic, but fans appreciated the campy quality. Blake had never worked with so much special effects makeup and fake blood, so it was definitely a challenge. But it was a fun challenge. Running and screaming all over the set with a bunch of other young, attractive actors and actresses was pretty cool. And between takes, Blake got the chance to spend some quality time with Kelly, Robyn and her husband Bart, Lori, and her dad. Blake's family has always been very close, and they treasured the time they got to spend together on set.

At the end of 2006, Blake changed things up again by taking the title role of "Anabelle" in the quirky independent film *Elvis and Anabelle* opposite Max Minghella as "Elvis." The sweet, heartwarming movie told the story of Anabelle, a Texas beauty queen whose pushy mother has been grooming her for stardom. After winning a beauty pageant, Anabelle collapses and dies on stage. Her body is sent to a funeral home where Elvis, the owner's son who has been forced to become a mortician, revives her with a spontaneous kiss. Neither of them is sure what happened, and the resulting media frenzy keeps them apart for a time. But Anabelle's death and revival have changed her. She finds herself drawn back to the funeral home where she and Elvis begin to really connect. When the media, police, and Anabelle's mother all become too much for the teens to bear, they take a road trip to the Texas coast and romance blossoms between them. But when a horrible tragedy brings them back home, the two must face everything they've been running from and redefine who they are. In the end, both teens find a happy ending and the film's overall message is incredibly positive.

Elvis and Anabelle premiered at the South by Southwest Music Festival in Austin, Texas, in early 2007, and then went on to several other film festivals. It won three awards at the Newport Beach Film Festival, including one for Blake for Breakout Performance. Blake had a great time exploring Texas and delving a little into her southern roots (Blake may have been born in California, but her family was originally from Georgia!). The character of Anabelle was very different from any role Blake had played before and it really gave her a chance to flex her acting muscles. She really loved perfecting her Southern accent and tackling such an emotional role. And working with Max Minghella was great for Blake. He also came from a prominent show business family, and the two clicked quickly. They became good friends and had a lot of fun together, but, despite all of that, Blake struggled with homesickness on the set. She missed her family, friends, and especially her boyfriend. As she explained to CosmoGirl.com, "I was away from L.A. for six weeks filming *Elvis and Anabelle.*

When my boyfriend and I had to say good-bye, we were like 'Oh six weeks, that's no big deal!' That only lasted five days; we've been back and forth seeing each other every week!" Blake's visits home helped keep her energy up and her performances fresh. And when Kelly visited Blake on set, they definitely took advantage of all Texas has to offer—including excellent barbecue, TexMex food, and great local music!

After finishing up *Elvis and Anabelle*, Blake turned her thoughts back to college. She was still on the lookout for choice film roles, but she didn't want her education to suffer in the process. But Blake had changed her mind about one big thing—Stanford. After filming on location in different places, doing press tours, and a little traveling, Blake had decided that she might want to try living on the East Coast for a while, just to give herself a broader perspective. "I'm hoping to start college courses this fall," Blake explained to CosmoGirl.com in 2007. "I want to go to NYU [New York University], at least for a while. I think it's a really important growing experience to live in New York. Living in a city makes you grow up and learn a lot, and I just think New York is the scariest city to be thrown into—it's, like, okay: live. I love New York so much. I can't wait!" Blake didn't know it then, but she was going to be heading to New York City in the fall, just not for college. Blake was going to have to put off school once again, but this time it was for the chance most young stars only dream of — a starring role in one of the most cutting-edge new shows on television.

Chapter 5: New York, Here She Comes

hile Blake was busy working on her film career, a new teen drama for the CW Network was being developed by Stephanie Savage and Josh Schwartz, the creator of the ultra successful teen drama *The O.C.* "I love to do stuff for this audience. When they're with you, they're incredibly passionate," Josh told *Vanity Fair* Daily. Josh's newest show was another teen drama, but this one was to be set in the über-exclusive world of New York City's Upper East Side. It was based on the *New York Times* bestselling *Gossip Girl* book series by Cecily von Ziegesar. The books were already incredibly popular with teens around the world, thanks in large part to the fantastically complex characters and outrageous plot twists, and so the show was sure to catch their attention.

Josh was inspired by Cecily's books, but he didn't want to copy them for the television show. Instead, he focused on taking the best parts of the books and using them as a jumping off point to create an incredibly cool show that would appeal to a larger audience. The result was a season's worth of scripts that were funny, smart, and a little scandalous. It took a lot of work to make sure the world and characters were perfect, but Josh and Stephanie were willing to put in the time and effort to get it right. "The books are pretty good, but beyond that, Stephanie spent some time in New York on the Upper East Side with some of these girls in real life and got the tour. We have writers who are from that world, so they bring a lot to the writing experience—a lot of flavor and texture that I think that makes it feel accurate in terms of geography, attitude, and tone. And then some of it is fantasy. Because we're not from that world, it gives us a little bit of an outsider perspective, which I think is helpful. Ideally you want people from that world to feel like we get it right, and people who aren't from that world to feel like they understand it and relate to it even though they haven't experienced it directly. That was our main task when we got to work on bringing the books to life. Plus, we wanted people to care about the characters despite the fact that they are incredibly rich and not always sympathetic," Josh explained to *Vanity Fair* Daily.

Once Josh and Stephanie had the scripts they wanted, it was time to cast the characters. It was a challenging process to find actors and actresses to fit the roles of the princes and princesses of the Upper East Side. Josh was very picky about who he cast, because he knew it wasn't going to be easy to make the privileged, devious, and spoiled characters likeable. He needed actors with the ability to tug at an audience's heartstrings, even when they were portraying bratty kids misbehaving. They auditioned hundreds of actors for the various parts, except when it came to the star role of "Serena van der Woodsen." Josh already knew exactly who he wanted for the part of Serena—Blake! But it took some serious convincing on Josh's part to sign Blake up for the role. Blake had never been interested in television, plus she had heard some of the more outlandish plot twists from the books and wasn't sure the show was going to be a serious enough role for her. "[I thought] if there are pet monkeys wearing coordinating outfits, that's not something I'm going to want to be a part of...." Blake told *Nylon* magazine. Eventually though, Josh won her over and Blake came on board as Serena. "Josh is very passionate, and he's very aggressive.

He called me personally on my cell phone, and he was like, 'You know, you have to do this, I wrote this for you, and I'm not going to do the show with anyone else, and I have to do the show, so you have to do it.' I've never wanted to do a TV show, just because you have to commit potentially six years of your life to something. It has to be something that you're really passionate about. But I met with them, and they are so excited about what they do. They are so passionate, they're young, and they're not some jaded studio executive who just signs off their name for some commercial product and goes to their house in the Hamptons and is never involved. They're involved from every outfit I wear to every person that gets cast, every backdrop of every scene. If I have a flyaway hair they come up and fix it for me. If it wouldn't have been them, I definitely don't think I'd be doing the show," Blake told BuzzSugar.com. After casting Blake, Josh and Stephanie chose model Leighton Meester to play queen bee "Blair Waldorf," hottie Chace Crawford for the role of cute but confused "Nate Archibald," British actor and singer Ed Westwick to play sleazy "Chuck Bass," brooding hunk Penn Badgley to take on sensitive "Dan Humphrey," and wide-eyed teen star Taylor Momsen to play his sister "Jenny Humphrey."

Connor Paolo signed on to play Serena's younger brother "Eric van der Woodsen," and Jessica Szohr also joined the cast as Dan's best friend "Vanessa Abrams." As for the show's adult characters, Kelly Rutherford from *The O.C.* was tapped to play "Lily van der Woodsen," Serena's mother, and Matthew Settle came on as "Rufus Humphrey," Jenny and Dan's dad.

With Blake on board and the rest of the cast in place, the show was poised to take off. There was just one more hurdle to overcome—the show's location. It was set in New York City, but the CW wanted to film it in Los Angeles for budget reasons and no one was happy about that. "It said on the sheet that they were shooting in L.A., so I thought 'That's gonna look silly. It'll be in the studio, and it's not going to read true.' And when I sat down with Josh and Stephanie, they were like 'We're doing it in New York.' I said 'Oh, have you gotten the approval from the studio?' They said 'No, they want to shoot in L.A., but we're doing it in New York!' And I totally believed them. I was like 'Yep, let's go to New York!' They got me very fired up," Blake told IGN TV. Josh and Stephanie eventually convinced the CW that the show would be more successful and believable if it was shot on location, so the entire cast and crew went to New York to film the pilot.

Filming the first episode of *Gossip Girl* was a blast for everyone involved. The cast really clicked and the result was an incredibly addictive and exciting new show. After seeing it, network executives instantly gave the go-ahead to shoot an entire season. "We're lucky, a lot of the stars aligned. The cast is really terrific and talented, and everybody's right for their parts, aside from being unbelievably attractive. New York and the Upper East Side seen through the eyes of young people is an exciting and seductive world. The use of technology and the way that these characters have built themselves into a self-inflicted fishbowl where their every action is blogged about, diagnosed, discussed, and gossiped about speaks to the way our celebrity culture is today and also the way people communicate with each other," Josh told *Vanity Fair* Daily. With the studio really pushing the new show, everyone scrambled to move to New York and get right to work. Blake was super excited, as she had already been wanting to live in New York. As she gushed to IGN TV, "I can't believe we're being paid to live in New York!"

Working on a television show was a new and challenging experience for Blake, but she loved it once she got started. "It's different character-wise because when you do a film, you have the character arc that you have to do in three months. You have to be a different person in the beginning than you are in the end. Whereas with one episode, you can't do the full range of who this person is because the TV show tells three days, where a movie can tell a whole summer or a year or a few years," Blake told BuzzSugar.com.

Blake's character, Serena, was very complex and it required a lot of emotional depth for Blake to portray her accurately. Serena is the reformed bad girl of the cast. She was a little wild in her past, and she hurt a lot of people with her selfish behavior. Then Serena realized that what she was doing was wrong, and went away to boarding school to clean up her act. The show picks up with Serena returning to New York City, her old school, and her old friends, where she must face all of the problems she ran away from before. "I think she's [Serena's] a really cool person. She's been brought up in this world where she's been taught that she can have anything she wants, like — 'Wear this pretty dress!' 'Go to this party!' 'If you want it take it!' 'You're the best!' ... All these kids, they're the center of their own universes. She realizes that that's bad, and I think that takes a good person, a strong person, to realize that. She comes back into this world and it would be so much easier for her to go back to her old ways because that's how everybody else is around her. They wouldn't think worse of her—they would accept her if she went and gossiped about everybody else. That would be great and easy. But she doesn't do that, and I think it's really important. She takes the criticism in order to do the right thing," Blake explained to BuzzSugar.com. It was very important to Blake that she get her character just right, because she felt like she, and a lot of other teens, could relate to Serena's predicament. "She's [Serena's] practically royalty, you know? The money that she's been surrounded by...But you know, people, whether they're very rich or poverty stricken, teens go through trials and tribulations and dramas, whenever you're finding out who you are. There are struggles. People gossip. People are insecure, so they talk about other people so that they won't be talked about. They point out flaws in other people to make them feel good about themselves. I think at any age or any social class that's present. So as far as that, I can relate to her, but her lifestyle, no way," Blake told IGN TV. Blake really went out of her way to get into Serena's head, and, as a result, her portrayal of the conflicted blonde bombshell is dead-on every time.

Blake loved that Josh and Stephanie wrote Serena as the heart and soul of *Gossip Girl*, but she was equally impressed with the thought they put into developing all of the other characters. Each role ended up having a very dynamic and interesting storyline that highlights the fact that the world is not black and white, which Blake feels is an important message to get out to viewers. "It was really neat to play such a complex character. Josh and Stephanie are really great at writing that. People aren't one-dimensional, because they're not in real life. I don't believe that there's a good guy and a bad guy. Unless it's like Superman or Batman, there is no good guy and bad guy. There are reasons that people are the way they are. Blair is vulnerable. You see her mother, and her mother is nitpicky on everything she does from her hair to her out-fits. 'You don't look skinny in that!' Her mother has made her feel insecure. Because she's insecure, she tells off her friend and is always trying to measure up. And it's not her fault. It's her mother; it's the way she was raised. My char-acter's mother was like 'Why don't you wear this to the party? Why don't you go out there? Why don't you dance on tables and look fabulous?' I was pushed too much to be free, and I thought 'Oh, I need to have whatever I want!' And I took my best friend's boyfriend, and it's not right. I think what's important is she realizes that it isn't right. That's a really great thing about Serena is you get to see a bit in flashback how she was a bit more wild and there's a moment where Blair is really beating up on Serena. She's always beating up on her, and there's a moment in the pilot where Serena says 'No, you *will* meet me here!' And she doesn't take no for an answer, and she gets strong for a second and you get an insight into what power she did have before and you see Blair be a little more vulnerable later. So I think it's really cool how complex they are," Blake told IGN TV. The show does tackle some very adult issues, and it has gotten some heat from critics for its sometimes racy storylines, but Blake feels that it's important to put some of those issues out there, because there are teens across the country living out those issues every day. "They [the Gossip Girl characters besides Serena] know there's another world out there, but they don't have to [go there] right now. They're indulging, they're living in the moment. They know they're going to end up like their parents, and they're going to have to run companies and be multimillionaires and have all these responsibilities and have children to take care of. But now they're young, and they're going to do what they want to do, and they have the privilege to do that. It takes a stronger person to be grown up right now," Blake told BuzzSugar.com. In response to the sometimes racy behavior of the show's characters, Blake just tries to stress that neither she, nor the rest of the cast, are like their characters. The world of *Gossip Girl* is extreme, entertaining, and interesting, but it is ultimately fictional, and Blake wouldn't encourage any of her fans to behave like the characters on the show!

The entire cast handled all of the complex issues and content with grace and maturity, and the result was that viewers were drawn to the show from the very beginning. *Gossip Girl* generated a lot of buzz before it even premiered, and when it did make its television debut, the response was explosive. Some critics loved it, some hated it, but the show's new fans were not to be swayed. Teens and young adults across the country began tuning in religiously, sucked in by the great writing, complex characters, and juicy plot twists. The show was quickly signed up for a second season, and if fans have anything to say about it, there will be many more seasons to come after that! And the media took to *Gossip Girl* and its cast just as quickly. Blake and her costars were named to *People's* Most Beautiful People List of 2008, and they picked up two wins for the show at the Teen Choice Awards of 2008 for Choice TV Show Drama, and Choice TV Breakout Show. A very excited Blake told *USA Today*, "It's so surreal to me because I remember sitting home watching the Teen

Choice Awards." Blake was even more excited when she discovered that she had won for Choice TV Actress Drama and Choice TV Breakout Star Female, while Chace Crawford won for Choice TV Breakout Star Male and Ed Westwick won for Choice TV Villain. *Gossip Girl* was officially a hit!

BLAKE LIVELY

BLAKE LIVELY

Chapter 6: Gossip

Sometimes life really does imitate art, and for the cast of *Gossip Girl* it wasn't long before they were as gossiped about as their characters. Fans were eager for news about their new favorite stars and the media was only too happy to oblige, running stories about tensions between cast members, on-set romances, and scandals galore! The paparazzi couldn't get enough of the hot new stars, and they followed them from location to location trying to dig up dirt. "Their cameras will be clicking during scenes while we're just trying to get through our lines. It sounds like a swarm of wasps," Blake told *Cosmopolitan*. The cast learned early on to avoid reading celebrity blogs and tabloids and just to ignore the rumors of tension on set, cat fights over wardrobe, and the actors dating and breaking up. But the stories still caught fans' attention, and the cast and crew have had to speak out to put those rumors to bed.

Blake doesn't actually have anything negative to say about her fellow stars, and she avoids gossiping in general. As she told *InStyle*, "If you gossip, it's going to come back at you." According to Blake and her castmates, most of the *Gossip Girl* drama takes place on-screen — not off!

In fact, Blake loves just about everything about filming *Gossip Girl*. Working on the show is largely drama-free for her. Blake loves living in New York City and working with the same people every day. Lots of the cast members live together or very close to each other, and they spend a lot of time together when they aren't working. That closeness has been especially nice for Blake because it has felt a little like going off to school. "We do everything together. It's like being freshmen in college," Blake explained to *Teen Vogue*. "I found my passion when I started acting, but I was sad that I had to miss out on school. So it's nice to have a collegiate experience." The cast goes to dinner and concerts together, and they take turns having game nights at each other's apartments. "You'd think we'd be sick of each other," Leighton Meester told *New York* magazine. "But we have so much fun." Blake is a huge fan of the game nights. Her all-time favorite game is Guitar Hero and she loves playing it with her friends. The show's writers even put a Guitar Hero segment into one of the episodes just for Blake. "The reason they wrote it in was because I'm such an amazing 'Guitar Hero' player. I saw clips of it. It doesn't really debut my skills so well, which I was very disappointed about," Blake explained to the Associated Press. One of the biggest rumors swirling about the show is that Blake and Leighton fight just as much as on-screen frenemies Serena and Blake. But, according to both girls, that just isn't true. Blake and Leighton get along very well and are often spotted grabbing lunch together on set or "ooohing" and "awing" over the gorgeous clothes and accessories in the wardrobe department. Blake thinks the press may have gotten the wrong idea because she is so focused on set that she isn't seen goofing around as much as some of the other actors. But it does happen. Even focused-and-professional Blake goofs off when she's done working for the day!

Blake has a ton of respect for her castmates. Not only are they all talented and dedicated actors, but they are all very genuine people and good friends. "Everyone is really funny and has such strange things that they do. Like Leighton does amazing voice impressions, and she can impersonate anyone's face. Chace does an amazing impression of Scott Stapp from Creed. Ed is always singing. Taylor is just so adorable, I just want to bake her a cupcake. And Penn does these silly dance moves, and he's very witty and quick, so it's fun to have sharp banter with him," Blake gushed to *Seventeen* magazine. Each of the cast members have very different personalities, which keeps everyone on their toes on set. Blake is more professional and serious while acting, Leighton is goofy and silly, Penn is clever and funny, and Ed is all about flirting. As he bragged to *New York* magazine, "Who is the most flirtatious? Definitely me! I'm a devil."

The comraderie and friendship on the set definitely helps smooth over the more awkward moments that can crop up when filming a drama like *Gossip Girl*. There are lots of love scenes on the show, which can be pretty strange to film, as Blake recounted to *Seventeen* magazine: "Chace and I had to do that scene in the first episode when I'm sitting on his lap on the barstool. Then they call, 'Cut!' and I just have to sit on the lap of this guy I met two weeks before! And I'm like, 'So, you want to get some pizza tonight or something?' What do you even talk about?!? It's not as romantic as people think it is." And when it comes down to it, those steamy kissing scenes are very fake! "Well, you don't actually make out. It's like fake kissing. When you make out for real, your lips and tongues touch. And when you make out on the show, it's just an open mouth. Your lips are touching each other, but there's definitely no kissing," Blake explained in the August 2008 issue of *Seventeen* magazine. "But nothing about kissing your costar is romantic...because you have forty crew members watching you. You have a director going, 'Tip your head to the right. To the left. Okay, now do this.' It's just awkward." Awkward or not, the cast does a great job of making those scenes very believable, probably because they have such great friendly chemistry with each other!

In some cases though, the fake love scenes have sparked some real romantic chemistry. Leighton briefly dated one of the guest-starring actors, and, midway through filming the first season of the show, romance blossomed between Blake and her on-screen love interest Penn Badgley. But it wasn't their scripted love scenes that brought the two together, as Blake explained to *Seventeen* magazine: "When you're saying these words [from the script] that people are making you say to one another, nothing about it is real or genuine. So if two people connect outside their characters, then that's how they get together." The two figured out pretty early on that they had a lot in common, and the more time they spent together, the more they clicked. Blake had broken up with her high school boyfriend shortly before moving to New York City, and wasn't exactly looking for another relationship, but Penn won her over. "He's [Penn's] very stoic and calm and confident. He's much more like Serena than I am," Blake bragged to *Cosmopolitan*. Blake and Penn both really respected and liked each other, so it wasn't a real surprise to anyone in the cast when they began dating. "I think she's incredible," Penn Badgley told *People*. "She's an amazing person and she's beautiful — so there's not a lot to dislike." As the two quietly started dating, rumors swirled about them, but the cast and crew were great at helping the new couple stay under the media radar. "They're both so together and whatever happens is their business, and I think they're both darling and very together as people," Kelly Rutherford explained to People.com. "To be able to go through this ride and success and to have somebody to do that with and share that experience, I think they're both very fortunate." The media finally confirmed the romance when they caught the couple smooching on vacation, but the two continue to keep a low profile about their love. Blake, always the professional, especially likes to keep the focus of her interviews on her work instead of gushing about her boyfriend.

Since the cast of *Gossip Girl* includes some of the hottest new stars in the industry and the show itself is centered on gossip and intrigue, rumors will probably continue to swirl about Blake and her friends. "It really does feel like we're living the show sometimes," Penn mused to *New York* magazine. "The psychology of celebrity is such a weird and new thing." Luckily, the cast members have great attitudes and can laugh off any bad press or crazy stories. And who knows, maybe the writers will take the real life rumors and work them into some of their scripts one of these days!

Chapter 7: Back in Blue Jeans

During the summer of 2007 Blake slipped back into a role that was as comfortable for her as, well, a pair of old blue jeans! She reprised her role of "Bridget Vreeland" in the film *The Sisterhood of the Traveling Pants 2*. Blake was incredibly excited to revisit the world of the magic blue jeans and the four friends they bring together. But she was even more excited to reunite with her co-stars, America Ferrera, Amber Tamblyn, and Alexis Bledel. "When we got back together, it was like no time had passed. We stayed together in two connecting suites, talked and sang...all night," Blake told *Teen Vogue*. The girls were psyched to be back together, but the sequel almost didn't happen. Producers weren't sure they could make it happen, but, at the last minute, it all came together. "The only thing that made any of us nervous was the fact that we had a six-week prep," Blake told *USA Today*. "It happened so fast. We were nervous because we didn't have a script at the beginning. We were all so happy to be together. We loved the first movie so much. We wanted to do a sequel. There was never any hesitation about that."

There was definitely lots of cheering, giggling, and goofing off when Blake, Amber, America, and Alexis got on set to film their scenes as a foursome. "When we get together now, we all just regress twenty years. We all act like one- and two-year-olds! We were singing Disney songs on the rooftops of buildings while we were filming in Greece, and we'd stay up all night talking. Even though we are all older now, we're all still the same people we were on the first movie," Blake explained to *Seventeen* magazine. Luckily, the girls' all-night singing antics didn't slow them down at all during filming. In fact, it only made their friendship that much stronger on screen! The girls got to film together in Greece, and they definitely had a good time exploring the beautiful country with Alexis, who had been there for the first film, as their knowledgeable tour guide. Blake thinks of America, Amber, and Alexis as big sisters, so it was very nice for her to get the chance to pick their brains for acting, boy, and friend advice, as well as learn from their considerable talents and skills once again.

The Sisterhood of the Traveling Pants 2 picks up a few years after the first film. All of the girls are off at college, pursuing their passions. Lena is studying art at the Rhode Island School of Design, but she has broken up with Kostas, her hunky Greek boyfriend. Carmen is trying to fit in at Harvard and has gotten involved behind the scenes at the theater program. Tibby is studying film at New York University and is still dating her high school boyfriend. And Bridget is on the varsity soccer team at Brown University and is studying archaeology. All of the girls are doing well at school, but the four friends have drifted apart since heading off to college, and their friendships are suffering, as Blake explained to IGN TV. "The first movie is so much about the Sisterhood and friendship, and we're doing our own things but we have this Sisterhood. But this next movie is three years later and we've grown up, we're adults. We're doing so many different things in our lives. We have boyfriends. We have family. We have soccer teams. We have so much going on and we're in different parts of the U.S., that we don't really have the Sisterhood so much. There's not so much time for it as there was before. So it's about us finding that again and it's hard. It's hard to make time and we kind of fall apart without our core, which is each other."

When none of the girls decide to stay home for the summer and their correspondence dwindles down to almost nothing, tensions between them reach an all-time high. Carmen heads off to a summer theater program where she snags the lead role in a play and the heart of a cute British actor. Lena discovers that Kostas has gotten married. She tries to move on by dating a fellow artist, but she just can't seem to get over her past love. Tibby is taking a summer class at NYU, but when a hasty decision ends her relationship with her boyfriend, she is at a loss as to what to do. And Bridget heads off to a school-sponsored archaeological dig in Turkey. But after discovering letters from her estranged grandmother, Bridget decides she needs to face her own past before she can study anyone else's. "My character, she has always been running away from dealing with her problems, namely her mother's suicide. She's in college and on the varsity soccer team at Brown and she's into archaeology now. So she goes off to a dig in Turkey, and she's looking at these bones of all these other people and finding out about all these other people's pasts, until she kind of realizes 'I need to deal with my own past!' and some things that really rock her. And she goes to her grandmother's, who she hasn't had a relationship with, ever, and really finds out about her mother and about her, because she never really knew her mother and her dad doesn't talk about it. So she's afraid 'Am I like her?' because she gets sad. But the reason she gets sad is because her mother killed herself! She just needs to hear 'You're a different person. I knew your mother. You're not sick, you're okay. And your mother did love you, she just had a problem.' So it's a really great realization for her," Blake explained to IGN TV. In the end, though, it isn't any of the girls' problems that bring them back together—it's the loss of the pants. And even that seems like part of the pants's magic, as the trip to Greece to search for them renews the girls' friendships and leaves them prepared to take on the world again.

Blake's role in *The Sisterhood of the Traveling Pants 2* was both physically and emotionally demanding. She played some soccer, fell through a hole and down into a buried room, and even managed to accidentally crash a moped in Greece—although that one was off camera! "...I was on crutches for three weeks, because I crashed a moped in Greece," Blake told IGN TV. "I've got a scar on the side of my leg." Blake took all of the physically demanding stuff (and the crutches!) in stride. Instead, she focused on the subtler emotional journey that Bridget goes on over the course of the film. Bridget struggles with lingering insecurities, emotions, and feelings of loneliness from her mother's suicide. She has dealt with them as well as she can, but she is also angry at her father and the rest of her family for not helping her mother. Bridget's trip to see her grandmother gives her a new perspective and helps her accept the fact that no one could have done anything more to help her mother. Accepting that fact allows Bridget to push forward, establish a relationship with her grandmother, and re-establish a closer relationship with her father. This time around, Blake could relate to what Bridget was going through even more than she could during the first film. "[Bridget] goes across the world, I was moving from Los Angeles to New York literally at the same time I was shooting this movie," Blake explained to *USA Today*. "I was moving away and starting out on my own. And I have these girls—people I work with, people on the show—that are really close." Being able to connect with and relate more strongly to her character definitely gave Blake an edge when it came to her performance. It wasn't easy to portray all of those emotions on screen, but Blake did a wonderful job handling them with subtlety and grace. Sanaa Hamri, the director of *The Sisterhood of the Traveling Pants 2* was especially impressed with Blake. As she told *USA Today*, "Blake is a young actor but very thorough. I can see why she's on the rise. Blake was such a big advocate of the Sisterhood. She loved Bridget. When she feels something is right, she follows her heart, no matter what. She's fearless and down-to-earth." Blake's performance is moving and easy to relate to, and her fans loved it.

Blake was excited to do the sequel because she loved her character, her co-stars, and the uplifting storylines and themes of the two films, but she really did the movie for her fans. There was such an overwhelming response to the first film that there was no way Blake could turn it down. The first film touched viewers in ways they hadn't expected, and it moved them to take action within their own lives. The fans' stories really inspired Blake, as she explained to IGN TV. "We deal with death. We deal with a broken family. We deal with loss of virginity. We deal with falling in love for the first time. Those are things that everyone can relate to and I know America said she brought one of her best guy friends to see the movie and he was so emotional about that and her storyline he con-nected to so much. He said 'This has happened with me and my father' and needed to call him. And I've had fathers come up to me and be like 'You know what? I was so selfish. I started this other family and I forgot. It was so much easier not to go back because I felt guilty, but this opened the door and now I have a relationship with my son.' People feel the need to tell us these personal things about their lives, which is really great, but for me it's shocking that people come up and give me such intimate details. The issues really are universal. I think that's what's so important about the film is it doesn't portray these young girls being superficial which so many movies do; girls just giggling and painting their toenails and talking about Zac Efron. But that's not how all girls are. A lot of people have to deal with real things, and you can get through it and you do need this good, moral center and friendship or family or whatever you need to get you through it. But you will get through it. Sorry, I'm preaching! But it's not about magical, dancing pants and I think the title scared a ton of people away. Almost every guy I talk to who's seen it has really enjoyed it," Blake said. Blake couldn't wait to give fans another film that built upon the emotion and resonance of the first film.

It seemed like the magic of the pants extended into the audience, because fans adored *The Sisterhood of the Traveling Pants 2*. Viewers left the theater touched, inspired, and in love with the characters all over again. It was the perfect good-bye for the fans, and for Blake and her co-stars who were saying good-bye to the roles that had brought them together. Luckily, they knew that their friendships would last as long as Lena, Carmen, Tibby, and Bridget's — all thanks to the traveling pants!

Chapter 8: Filming Future

Blake is never one to take a lot of time off between projects, so she managed to film two movies during the summer of 2008, between shooting season one and season two of *Gossip Girl*. The first was a small role in the ensemble picture *New York, I Love You* and the second was the role of "Young Pippa Lee" in *The Private Lives of Pippa Lee*. Both films marked a dramatic departure from *Gossip Girl* in tone and subject matter, which was a nice change for Blake. The films also gave Blake a chance to work with some serious Hollywood heavyweights.

New York, I Love You is the follow up film to *Paris, je t'aime*. *Paris, je t'aime* is a French film made up of eighteen five-minute shorts, each of them focusing on a love story set in Paris. *New York, I Love You* follows the same format—with twelve international directors directing twelve short love stories set in New York City. "*New York,*

I Love You is a true testament to one of the greatest cities in the world," Marina Grasic, one of the film's producers, explained to PalmPictures.com. "I am personally honored to work with such an esteemed cast and some of the foremost filmmakers in the world." The film's directors are Mira Nair, Yvan Attal, Andrei Zvyagintsev, Albert and Allen Hughes, Joshua Marston, Fatih Akin, Jiang Wen, Brett Ratner, Shunji Iwai, Shekhar Kapur, Natalie Portman, and Scarlett Johansson. The shorts star some of the biggest names in Hollywood, including Natalie Portman, Orlando Bloom, Christina Ricci, Shia LaBeouf, Julie Christie, John Hurt, Hayden Christensen, Rachel Bilson, Chris Cooper, Drea de Matteo, Ethan Hawke, Kevin Bacon, Olivia Thirlby, and, of course, Blake!

Blake was completely psyched to land a role in such an illustrious production, especially since it was being filmed in the city she has fallen in love with herself. And since she was in such a short segment, it didn't take her very long to film her portion. Blake played the role of "Girlfriend" in the movie, and she completely nailed her part. It was a very small role, but Blake was just honored to have made the cut alongside such other incredible actresses and actors.

The entire film was shot in just thirty-six days and has been dedicated to Anthony Minghella, the father of Blake's *Elvis and Anabelle* co-star Max Minghella. Anthony was to have directed one of the shorts titled "Upper East Side," but he passed away before he could finish. When Anthony realized he was not going to make it, he asked Shekhar Kapur to replace him. Shekhar was honored to take over for Anthony, as he wrote in his blog: "I will direct the film now — with Anthony in my heart and in presence of his soul." The entire cast and crew were devastated by the news of Anthony's death, and they were all pleased by the producer's decision to dedicate the film to him. Blake was especially supportive of the dedication, as she and Max Minghella had become very close while filming *Elvis and Anabelle*, and she knew how difficult it was for him to say good-bye to his father. She must have been very proud to be a part of the film industry's official celebration of Anthony.

After filming wrapped on *New York, I Love You*, Blake headed to Connecticut to film *The Private Lives of Pippa Lee*. The film was written by the critically acclaimed writer Rebecca Miller, daughter of famed American playwright Arthur Miller. The film is based on Rebecca's debut novel of the same name. Blake was thrilled to work with such a beautiful script, and couldn't wait to tackle the emotional film. Her role was challenging and her character deals with some very adult issues in the film. Blake was a little concerned about taking on a more adult role, but she felt it was important for her to take the part because it would give her a chance to really flex her acting muscles. She doesn't want to alienate any of her younger fans, but Blake is always working to challenge herself and push her talents to new levels, even if it means taking on a part that might not appeal to everyone.

The Private Lives of Pippa Lee tells the story of Pippa Lee, a fifty-year-old woman whose life is shattered when her older husband leaves her for a younger woman. Pippa, devastated by her husband's infidelity, begins to delve into her memories and re-examine her life's path. Pippa had not had an easy life. She ran away from her drug-addicted mother when she was seventeen, and struggled with her own drug issues and bad relationships. After a period of self-examination, Pippa eventually finds a sense of security and purpose again in her grown children. "The book is about how changeable identity is and the extent to which anyone person is consistent," Rebecca Miller explained to nadineoregan.wordpress.com. "The lead character, Pippa, is based on someone I met up with who I hadn't met in a long time. She was a girl who was wild in her youth." Blake played young, wild "teenage Pippa" and Robin Wright Penn played "adult Pippa." Julianne Moore, Winona Ryder, Alan Arkin, Monica Bellucci, Maria Bello, and Keanu Reeves also starred in the film. Blake was super excited to work alongside such accomplished actors and actresses. She hopes to be the type of long-lasting, dynamic film actress that both Julianne Moore and Robin Wright Penn personify, so Blake was probably taking lots of mental notes while she watched them perform.

One of the best things about playing Pippa was the outrageous hair, makeup, and costumes Blake got to wear. Her hair was curled and teased, she wore bright red lipstick and heavy eye makeup, and her costumes were made up heavily of animal prints and leather. All of Blake's scenes took place in the 1970's, so her costumes were retro and rebellious. Young Pippa's look was very different from the usual designer duds Blake rocks as Serena on *Gossip Girl*, and Blake had a blast changing it up. It's always fun to play dress up on set, and since Blake has never been one to dress too outrageously in her personal life, playing Pippa was extra fun!

Since most of *The Private Lives of Pippa Lee* was filmed in Connecticut, it was easy for Blake to commute back and forth from the set to her home in New York. It was an ideal situation for Blake since she didn't want to miss out on all of the fun in New York City or leave behind her friends and boyfriend, Penn Badgley, for the summer! It also meant that Blake was easily accessible to the *Gossip Girl* crew for fittings and publicity events in preparation for filming season two of the hit show, which made just about everyone happy with Blake's filming schedule.

Both *New York, I Love You* and *The Private Lives of Pippa Lee* were departures for Blake compared to the roles she has taken on in the past. But she's hoping that choosing two such critically anticipated films with such strong casts will help propel her from a young actress to a true leading lady over the next few years. From the way things are going, it wouldn't seem like Blake has anything to worry about. She's already well on her way to being a star with true staying power!

Chapter 9: Looking Forward

Blake is, by far, one of the fastest rising young stars in Hollywood. With her gorgeous looks, considerable acting skills, and dynamic résumé of roles, it's no surprise that all eyes are on Blake to see what this surprising starlet will do next. One thing is certain though, no matter what Blake chooses for her next project, it will inevitably be a success!

There are a few givens for Blake over the next few years. She will continue to wow fans as Serena van der Woodsen on *Gossip Girl*. Season two is already keeping viewers on their toes, and season three is sure to be even better! Serena is a wonderfully deep and complex character, and Blake has a lot to work with over the next few seasons. Blake will also, no doubt, continue to evolve as a fashion icon. Between her ultra-cool personal style and Serena's flawless fashion sense, Blake is poised to become the Sarah Jessica Parker of her generation. Fans can't get enough of Blake and her fashion-forward choices. And just like Carrie Bradshaw before her, Serena van der Woodsen has become a character that personifies New York style. Blake has amazing taste and is often spotted in the coolest designer boutiques. She is also becoming a familiar face at fashion shows, and magazines are lining up to have her model the hottest new looks on their pages. *Vanity Fair* has already named Blake one of the "it girls" of "Hollywood's New Wave" along with Kristen Stewart, Emma Roberts, and Amanda Seyfried, claiming that "Boundaries dissolve everywhere they turn their pretty heads."

Blake will also continue to pursue her film career while on breaks from filming *Gossip Girl*. She knows that she wants to have a long-lasting career rich with variety, which means that Blake will be taking on a wide range of roles. She has already tackled a number of difficult parts, and that's not likely to change anytime soon. Blake chooses her projects very carefully, and she won't take a role unless she is truly passionate about a film and it's message. Blake will never accept a starring role in a film just because she thinks it will be successful; she's actually much more likely to take a small part in what she believes will be an important film, even if it's never likely to be a huge hit! With her talent and dedication, directors are eager to work with Blake, so she'll have no shortage of projects to pick from!

For now, though, Blake is just focusing on living a semi-normal life, despite her newfound fame. "It's pretty crazy. Not only [as] Serena van der Woodsen, but people know my own name. . . . [Everyone] from young girls, teenage girls, women in their thirties and forties to, like, . . . like frat boys. One day these, . . . guys were, like, coming out, rolling out of their Escalade and they go—they're like, 'Man, that's Gossip Girl!' And they were, like, freaking out. It was so strange how many people would just get giddy over it. And it's people that you would not expect at all," Blake told the Associated Press. Luckily, she's getting the hang of flying under the radar. She stays out of the limelight as much as possible, unless she's promoting her show or a new project. And Blake has become an expert at keeping interviews and publicity outings focused on her work instead of personal life. She keeps her private life as hush hush as possible—she won't even tell reporters which Manhattan neighborhood she lives in! Blake wants to keep a low profile, but there are some perks to being famous. Blake now has a much larger pool of roles to choose from and directors can't wait to work with her! She also loves going to premieres and events and meeting people that she's looked up to since she was little. Blake does admit that even she gets a little starstruck from time to time, even though she's a star herself. "It is a crazy and completely insane business. I'll go to an event...and I'll walk around and meet people who I always thought were such a big deal," Blake explained to *CosmoGIRL!*

At the end of the day, Blake just wants to be happy. She's pursuing her passion, spending lots of time with friends and family, and having a blast living her life. There are other dreams she wants to pursue in the future, like going to college, but for now she is completely focused on becoming the kind of actress that her fans can respect and relate to—both on screen and off!

Chapter 10: Blake Behind the Scenes

When Blake isn't lighting up the big screen or strutting her stuff on the red carpet, she's actually a completely low-key girl. Blake likes to leave all of the drama in her life at work. When she's performing, Blake is all about professionalism and focus. She gives 110 percent of her energy to her work. So when she's off the clock, Blake prefers to take it easy.

Blake enjoys being a stay-at-home type of girl. She loves curling up on the couch with yummy take-out and watching the Food Network. She also loves spending time rearranging her furniture and adding new accessories to her already well-designed apartment. "I would love to open my own interior decorating business. I grew up reading Martha Stewart and Williams-Sonoma catalogs, I was never interested in things like *Teen Beat*," Blake told *Lucky* magazine. And nothing cheers Blake up more when she's down than freshly baked treats and flowers. "Baking and flower arranging have always been my favorite hobbies," Blake told *Teen Vogue*. Blake also loves putting on music and dancing around her apartment, or just relaxing to one of her favorite albums at the end of a hard day at work. "My favorite music is Ray Charles for when I want to feel mellow, and Britney Spears or Justin Timberlake when I want something more funky," Blake told *Lucky* magazine.

Blake spends a lot of time hanging out with her friends, family, and boyfriend, Penn Badgley. "They [my family] are my best friends, anything that goes wrong I go to them. I'm not a wild person at all. You never read about me dancing on a banquette at some club because that never happens," Blake told *Teen Vogue*. Blake would never be described as a party girl. She's more interested in spending time with her friends than she is in dancing or drinking. "I don't drink, so when you're going out to a really loud place, where you can't talk to other people, and people are drinking, you can't really have a conversation. I just never really found much joy in it. Especially if there's something else fun to do, like play Guitar Hero," Blake explained to

Seventeen magazine. But Blake's favorite thing to do with her time off is to go shopping and explore her new home, New York City.

Moving to New York City was a dream of Blake's, and now that she's living there, she's taking advantage of everything the city has to offer. She's often spotted strolling through the West Village, SoHo, and the trendy Meatpacking District with her adorable dog, Penny. She loves sampling all of the wonderful restaurants that Manhattan offers, especially the great sushi spots! "On average, I order about three meals for myself in one sitting," Blake told *Cosmopolitan*. Blake is definitely a star who isn't afraid to have a big meal! She loves pasta, bread, cheese, and, her all-time favorite, dessert! After a delicious meal, Blake can usually be spotted checking out all of the amazing boutiques and big designer stores. New York City offers some of the best shopping in the country, and Blake definitely takes advantage of that! She also adores going to Broadway shows, especially Broadway revivals that she grew up loving. "I'm a huge *Rent*-head," Blake admitted to VanityFair.com. "I met Adam Pascal the other night and I got all goofy and weird."

Blake doesn't see herself as a big star. She works hard to advance her career, but that's just her job. At the end of the day, she still gets starstruck from time to time, like when she meets people like Adam Pascal and Angelina Jolie. "The people I look up to do very serious character roles," Blake told *New York* magazine. Blake doesn't think that she could ever be as glamorous as someone like Angelina. "People think I'm goofy. I don't have the whole Angelina Jolie air to me. I wish that I did, and that's an insecurity of mine," Blake explained to *Cosmopolitan*. It's strange to think that a beautiful starlet like Blake has days when she doesn't feel so beautiful—but she's just like every other girl who has insecurities every now and then. Especially when the tabloids and media say negative things about her. Luckily for Blake, most of the time she's happy just the way she is! "If you pay attention to what everyone else thinks, you're going to be forever unhappy. It's a happy person who doesn't waste their time with pettiness and negativity. All that really matters is that the people you care about think of you highly," Blake explained to *Seventeen* magazine.

Blake is lucky enough to have some incredible people in her life who love and support her through everything. She is very close with her parents, and her brothers and sisters. They all respect and love each other very much. Blake's sister Robyn even named her son Wyatt Blake

Johnson in honor of Blake! Blake also has a small, but very close group of friends that she would do anything for. "... I don't have friends just to have friends. I have a small group of people I truly love with all my heart," Blake explained to *Seventeen* magazine. Blake does have one special love of her life—her three-year-old maltipoo, Penny. Blake named her adorable pooch after "Penny" from the Disney animated classic *The Rescuers*. Having Penny with her wherever she goes helps Blake feel grounded and at home, even when she's halfway around the world on a set! "She eats bones and stuff. She's a real dog," Blake told *USA Today*. "I bring her with me everywhere. It's nice to have another heartbeat. She's a little piece of home."

With such a loving family, loyal dog, and supportive group of friends, Blake can afford to be very picky when it comes to letting new people into her life. "I haven't been in many relationships. I don't want to date someone just to date someone. I want to be with a guy who's going to better my quality of life and better me," Blake told *Cosmopolitan*. "A guy's also perfect if he doesn't try to eat my dessert." Blake has actually only ever kissed three boys off screen! But when Blake began spending time with her *Gossip Girl* co-star Penn Badgley, she knew she had found a guy who would make her life better in every way. "I'm the happiest I've ever been. When I'm in a relationship, I give my heart and soul to it and do it a hundred percent," Blake explained in *Cosmopolitan*. She and Penn began dating quietly midway into filming season one, and they've been pretty inseparable ever since. Blake isn't in any hurry to settle down and get married, but she really loves Penn and is having a great time dating him. They share lots of the same views and they both love doing the same things. "If a guy can play Guitar Hero with me and sit at home and watch the Food Network and read magazines with me, that's good. I don't think there are many guys that's fun for. It's a lot to ask," Blake joked to *Cosmopolitan*.

Blake and Penn both love playing Guitar Hero, although Blake is definitely the bigger fan! Guitar Hero is a video game that pits player against player to see who can rock harder on a special guitar-shaped controller. Blake just happens to be amazing at the game! "I play in tournaments in Brooklyn. I'll cover myself in [fake] sailor tattoos and dress like a rock star. Everyone else dresses totally normally and must think I'm a complete freak! I'll play with people there or my friends," Blake told *Seventeen* magazine. She always chooses to play as "Pandora! She's kind of bossy," Blake explained to *Seventeen* magazine. Her favorite song to play? "I like Ozzy Osbourne's 'Bark at the Moon,'" Blake told *Seventeen* magazine. Guitar Hero also gives Blake an excuse to get together with her *Sisterhood of the Traveling Pants* co-star and fellow New Yorker, America Ferrera, who is also a huge Guitar Hero fan. "One of my favorite pastimes to do while I'm at work in-between setups is to play Guitar Hero," America told *USA Today*. Playing games like Guitar Hero is a great way for Blake to hang out with her friends and goof off!

While Blake likes to live her personal life out of the spotlight, she likes to grab attention when she's promoting a new project or encouraging fans to check out her television show. But, at the end of the day, Blake is just a laid-back California girl who wants to hang out with her family and friends and enjoy her life without being constantly scrutinized. Which is why Blake is so thankful for her fans, who seem to understand and respect Blake's need for privacy when she's off the clock. Blake is never going to be a star who is constantly in the media for her crazy antics or diva-like behavior. She is much more likely to be known for her acting talents, gorgeous looks, fashion sense, and, of course, her killer Guitar Hero skills!

Chapter 11: Fashionably Blake

Blake is a rising star in the acting world, but she's also an up-and-coming style icon in the fashion world. Designers love working with the striking and leggy blonde, and her fans love her eclectic style — both on and off camera! Blake takes her style cues from some of the greatest fashionistas of all time, but she also puts her own, completely irresistible spin on her looks. "My style has been totally influenced by Audrey Hepburn and Kate Moss equally — they're such fashion icons. But Sienna Miller's young, urban style is also totally what I'm going for," Blake told *Lucky* magazine. Between her role as Upper East Side princess and her own edgy blend of California casual and New York downtown chic, Blake is about as fashion-forward as a star can get. She doesn't play it safe when it comes to her look, and her risky fashion statements are making waves and putting her squarely on most "best dressed" lists!

Blake absolutely adores fashion and she loves shopping. And moving to New York City, the fashion capital of America, has certainly upped Blake's shopping game. "I grew up in Southern California, so the whole concept of winter is this entirely new, exciting thing for me — I've already justified buying seven coats!" Blake explained to *Lucky* magazine. Blake hits up the big designer shops as much as possible in New York. Her favorites are "Jimmy Choo and Chanel. I can't stand it: the security guards know me there," Blake told *Vanity Fair*. But the designer shops in the posh SoHo neighborhood are only the start for this New Yorker. Blake also spends a lot of time browsing through the tiny boutiques of up-and-coming designers that dot the streets and storefronts of the East Village and West Village. There she can find funky, cool, cutting-edge dresses, bags, and tops. Blake is a true individual, so it's important to her that her look is as unique as she is. She wouldn't want to be seen wearing the same dress as four other girls, she likes to keep her look one-of-a-kind!

So how does she create her distinctive style? By pairing basics from her favorite lines — like J Brand skinny jeans or tank tops from C&C California — with something truly one-of-a-kind or higher end. Blake's everyday favorites include skinny jeans, basic tank tops, vests, slouchy boots, big leather bags, preppy dresses, cropped jackets, and long necklaces. Blake doesn't have to watch a budget when shopping for clothes — which is her favorite perk about being an actress — but that doesn't mean she always spends a fortune on her looks, and you don't have to either! You can get Blake's favorite basics at affordable prices. They sell skinny jeans, tank tops, vests, and slouchy boots at tons of stores where you don't have to pay designer prices. And once you have the basics, it's easy to find special accessories or extra pieces that are as unique as you are. Save your money and splurge on a long, layered necklace, or a special bag that goes with everything, or an amazingly cool vest that no one else will be wearing! Those little touches will help you stand apart from the crowd, just like Blake!

Blake's everyday look may be casual, but she can't hit the red carpet wearing jeans and a tank top. Normally she hates making too much of a fuss over her clothes, but she does love dressing up for a special event every once and a while. So when it's time for a more formal event, Blake goes all out. And, luckily for Blake, designers are more than happy to help her create the perfect look for any occasion. Designers are very inspired by Blake, and lots of them make sure she has front row seats at their fashion shows at Fashion Week in Paris and New York. So what does Blake go for when she's getting dressed up? Dresses, of course! Blake has amazing long legs and she likes to show them off. Mini-dresses and short skirts look great on her, and she loves wearing them! Blake likes to take big risks, wearing a lot of high-concept dresses that would look a little odd on anyone except her. She can pull off some pretty outrageous looks, like a bright green satin dress with a puffy skirt and a sweetheart neckline or a sleek cocktail dress with a blue velvet skirt and a plaid, draped top with leather detailing. Despite taking risks with fabrics and new designers, Blake does stick to classic silhouettes, and she tries not to show too much skin, "I'm having so much fun, but I'm trying to keep my head together too, style-wise. There are so many young women out there dressing like young girls; I want to be more lady-like and classic," Blake told *Lucky* magazine. Blake takes big risks because she knows how to have fun with fashion. She's never worried about some reporter disliking her out-fit. She chooses her outfits because they make her feel good about herself and she has a great time wearing them — not because someone else likes the way she looks. And

Blake would probably encourage all of her fans to have fun with their clothes, too, especially when it comes to a special occasion! As long as you feel fantastic in what you are wearing, then you are sure to have a great time, even if your look is completely different than anyone else's.

To complete any of her stylish looks, Blake accessorizes with cool jewelry and, of course, hair and makeup. She loves chunky bangle bracelets and long, layered necklaces, but Blake tends to keep her jewelry on the sparse side. She doesn't like to overaccessorize, so each piece that she does wear is extra-special! For her hair, Blake likes a pretty natural look. She sometimes adds long blonde hair-extensions to add length and volume to her own already-long hair, and she wears them in loose waves or a messy up-do. But for fancier occasions, Blake lets her stylist go crazy. She's been spotted with highly teased hair, smooth, lady-like French twists and buns, and long, straight locks. Blake usually keeps her make-up simple. She has creamy, flawless skin that she plays up with a little blush, some softly smoky eye makeup, and shiny lip gloss. But for dressy nights out, Blake plays up her looks with heavier eye makeup and deep red lips.

As an actress, Blake doesn't always get to dress the way she would like to. When playing a role, she has to take on the fashion choices of her character. Her role as Bridget Vreeland in *The Sisterhood of the Traveling Pants* and *The Sisterhood of the Traveling Pants 2*, had Blake exploring the worlds of sportswear and eclectic, global travel wear. In the first film, Bridget was usually outfitted in soccer gear, including running shorts, and supportive tank tops. For the second film, Bridget gravitated more towards practical clothing with eccentric details. She wore lots of tank tops and tunics with beading and embroidery in earthy colors, linen pants and shorts, and vests and pants with cargo pockets. She accessorized her looks with carved wooden bracelets and necklaces made out of hemp and wooden beads. Bridget's clothing in the film gives a lot away about her personality. It's easy to see just from looking at her that she is sporty, loves to travel, and is extremely practical.

Blake's most well-known role as Serena van der Woodsen couldn't be more different from the role of Bridget when it comes to fashion. Serena is a wealthy, Upper East Side Manhattan socialite, and she has money to burn when it comes to her wardrobe. Practically everything Serena wears, with the exception of her school uniform, has a high-end designer label attached to it. Serena actually wore a $12,000 John Galliano jacket and a $10,000

Chanel coat for her first day of school! But, most critics agree, Serena's taste, or rather the taste of the *Gossip Girl* wardrobe staff, is immaculate. All of Serena's clothing is chosen by Eric Daman, who also worked on the wardrobe for *Sex and the City*, and his assistant, Meredith Markworth-Pollack. Blake has a lot of respect for the two, and she has learned a lot about fashion from working with them. "Blake personally blames Eric for her new shopping addiction. She'll bring in her own Burberry bag and wear it on the show. We have a constant bartering system — it works out great," Meredith explained to *Vanity Fair*.

Serena's look is, at times, similar to Blake's own, because Meredith and Eric have been inspired by Blake's personality and because Blake has been inspired by Serena's sense of style. However, unlike Blake, Serena never wears the same thing twice. She is always at the forefront of the fashion scenes, wearing the newest, hottest, trendiest looks. On the show, Serena is trying to shake her wealthy, spoiled princess image so her look has a little bit of downtown grunge thrown into it, and she almost always looks a little thrown together, like she isn't trying too hard. She loves tight jeans, short skirts, leather vests and jackets, sparkly or beaded tops, and of course, the most eye-catching bags out there. She also likes clothes that have a bohemian chic edge, like linen dresses with embroidery or flowy beaded tunic tops. But it's easier than people might think to copy Serena's look from the show without spending a fortune! "Have fun with it like Jenny Humphrey does, and listen to your fashion sense. Go to a vintage or thrift store and have it tailored so it looks like Marc Jacobs. Forever 21 does great knockoffs, but it's all about individuality," Eric and Meredith advised *Vanity Fair*. Serena has great taste, but she's definitely a character that doesn't place too much emphasis on her looks. She's the only *Gossip Girl* character likely to show up at school with unwashed hair and no makeup, but somehow she manages to look pretty perfect anyway! Serena's advice to anyone who wanted to copy her look would probably be to mix it up. She would definitely encourage girls to take chances with new trends and have fun doing it, much like what Blake does in her personal style!

The *Gossip Girl* costume designers were inspired by real-life stars and New York City socialites to create the perfect look for Serena and her friends. "For Serena, it's Kate Moss. She has that thrown together, roll-out-of-bed appearance, but always looks incredible, which is really hard to do. For Blair, it's Audrey Hepburn and Anna Wintour — always classic, impeccably well kept, and has been working on her look for years," Eric and Meredith explained to *Vanity Fair*. "If you put Blair and Serena together, you get Tinsley Mortimer. Tinsley's hair is always set and she always looks perfect, but she takes risks. We also incorporate Arden Wohl's downtown doyenne look — headbands, floral dresses, and chunky shoes. As for the *Gossip* boys, socialite Derek Blasberg was the paradigm with his bow ties, classic squares, and sneakers. We were worried whether Middle America would get it, but then we saw a teenage boy — a fan hoping to catch a glimpse of the cast — waiting outside The Palace Hotel for hours wearing Chuck's signature J. Press scarf, so clearly people relate." Picking the perfect looks for Serena, Blair, Chuck, and Nate was much easier than styling characters like Vanessa, the Brooklyn hipster, and Lily van der Woodsen, Serena's mother and former rock band groupie. "Vanessa is a breath of fresh air. She's the Lower East Side, *Raising Victor Vargas* home girl. One night we saw M.I.A. in concert wearing a sequin sailor suit and were like 'Omigod, she is *so* Vanessa,'" Eric and Meredith explained to *Vanity Fair*. "As for Lily, who is played by Kelly Rutherford, we are very into Madonna, pre-*Hard Candy*, with a little Ivana Trump mixed in. Kelly comes from that world, and she's like 'I have a Birkin and a Kelly, so I can just use both,' and we're like 'Um, OK!' " Eric and Meredith are very inspired by pop culture phenomena and the cutting-edge independent music scenes in New York. They are constantly on the look out for new street style that hasn't gone mainstream yet, and is sure to inspire viewers!

Creating the perfect looks for all of the *Gossip Girl* characters was a challenge, even for two experienced costume designers like Eric and Meredith. Their budget isn't big enough to outfit so many fashionable characters in the pricey designer clothing that they would wear, and that was a big problem early on in the show. Most television shows don't have a large enough wardrobe budget, but designers often lend clothing to shows. Having their looks on television is like free advertising, so both the designers and the shows win. However, it took a little while before designers were willing to loan *Gossip Girl* their clothing. "In the beginning people were like, 'We don't know what this show is.' But after three episodes, the tables totally turned and now Valentino is begging to send us stuff. Van Cleef and Arpels just sent us a necklace worth a million dollars—it comes with its own security!" Eric and Meredith explained to *Vanity Fair*. Now that Eric and Meredith have plenty of designer backing, they have their pick of the litter. Their favorites? "Phillip Lim always looks smart and put together, and we love Brooks Brothers' new Black Fleece line. Alexander Wang, Vena Cava, Lorick, and Ralph Lauren are also fantastic. And Gemma Redux makes these amazing drippy serpentine necklaces and bracelets. Henri Bendel *is Gossip Girl*, but we also hit up Intermix, Opening Ceremony, and THECAST," Eric and Meredith told *Vanity Fair*. Eric and Meredith's planning has certainly paid off. "...with *Gossip Girl* people react to full looks, like, 'I want to be a Blair,' or 'I want to be a Serena.' It's a whole lifestyle. *Gossip Girl* does have quintessential items though: tights and headbands. Falke makes great tights, but we'll also go to H&M and grab every color. [Former *V.F.* staffer] Stacey Lapidus and Cara Couture do the best headbands," Eric and Meredith explained to *Vanity Fair*. Fans of the show across the country are scouring stores to copy the looks they see on the show — and who can blame them? Blake and her friends always look incredible!

You'd think that Blake, Leighton Meester, Taylor Momsen, and Jessica Szohr would be used to getting dressed in the coolest clothes every day to shoot their scenes, but they are still just as excited as they were on the first day of filming! "Everybody comments on each other's clothes. You have to say 'cute' five times when you enter the set!" Leighton explained to *New York* magazine. You can't really blame them though. Their clothes are *super* cute! With all of those incredible outfits around all day, it would be hard not to be inspired stylistically. "Growing up, I was constantly borrowing clothes from my older sisters, or I'd pick out something from Urban Outfitters and my mom would tailor it to my size — I don't think I ever dressed like a kid. Now that I'm on *Gossip Girl*, the wardrobe is so amazing and inspiring, it's opened a whole new style gateway for me!" Blake told *Lucky* magazine.

Whether she's getting sporty as Bridget, inspiring gossip on the Upper East Side as Serena, hanging out and shopping downtown with her pup, Penny, or glamming it up on the red carpet, Blake truly is a fashion icon for her generation. She is one of the only actresses her age who manages to rock the fashion world with every outfit she wears. Her style continues to evolve, and her fans and the media can't get enough of her eclectic choices. And everyone is waiting anxiously to see where her style choices will head next!

Chapter 12: Becoming Blake

Blake is undeniably a rising star and a brilliant actress. One of the things that makes her such a star is that she has the ability to find a little bit of herself in every role she plays—no matter how different that character might seem on the surface! Want to find out which of Blake's characters you're most like? Take this "Becoming Blake" quiz to find out!

1.) You need to study for a big test, but there is an amazing party going on. What do you do?

    a.) You try to study, but you let your friends talk you into going to the party.

    b.) You head to the party for a little while and then go home early to study.

    c.) You gather your best girlfriends so you can all study together and then get ready and go to the party together, too.

    d.) You study. Then, only if you have time, you go to the party for a little while.

2.) You go shopping for a big night out. What type of outfit do you choose?

 a.) A fabulous designer mini dress, stiletto heels, and a cropped leather jacket

 b.) A lace trimmed camisole, jean skirt, and flip flops

 c.) Your lucky jeans, a sporty but flirty tank top, and comfy shoes for dancing

 d.) A tube top, skinny jeans, a funky trench coat, and a pair of amazing boots from Chanel

3.) You and your best friend have a huge fight on the phone. How do you handle it?

 a.) You give her time to cool off. Then, when she's ready to talk, you race to her side to work things out.

 b.) You call back and apologize right away. You hate fighting with your friends.

 c.) You drop everything to go to her house and make things right.

 d.) You turn to your family for advice.

4.) You have a huge crush on a boy. How do you get his attention?

 a.) You invite yourself along to hear his dad's band play when he mentions it.

 b.) You show up at a party he's throwing and dance with him all night.

 c.) You impress him with your soccer skills and then challenge him to a race after practice.

 d.) You hang out with him away from the rest of your friends so that he has a chance to focus on your incredible personality.

5.) Your perfect boy would be:

a.) A little bit of an outsider with a great sense of humor who is also a hopeless romantic

b.) A quirky independent thinker who likes a challenge

c.) An adorable jock who also happens to be smart and cute

d.) A low-key, artsy guy that you have a lot in common with

6.) Your ideal pet would be:

a.) A goldfish. They don't allow anything bigger where you live.

b.) A pet rock — they are way more unique than any other type of pet!

c.) A golden retriever you've had since you were little

d.) An adorable, tiny dog that fits right in your purse

7.) After high school, what do you plan to do?

a.) Head to an Ivy League school with all of your best friends.

b.) Go to a good local college to major in media studies, although you aren't opposed to transferring to a less traditional school down the road!

c.) Get a soccer scholarship to a college with a great study abroad program and major in archaelogy.

d.) Put off college for a few years (even though you really want to go) to pursue acting.

8.) Your extra-curricular activities include:
    a.) Getting all you can out of your city. You love going to art galleries, hearing bands play, and, of course, shopping with your friends
    b.) Taking pictures for the school newspaper
    c.) Sports
    d.) Cheerleading, show choir, and student government

9.) When you grow up, you would like to be a:
    a.) You aren't sure, but you want to help people in some way
    b.) Photographer
    c.) Archaeologist
    d.) Actress

10.) How would you most like to spend your summer vacation?
    a.) Hanging out at a fabulous beach with your best friends
    b.) Traveling across America taking pictures
    c.) At a sports camp
    d.) Filming an independent movie

Blake's *Gossip Girl* character "Serena van der Woodsen" is a reformed bad girl. She was brought up in an extremely wealthy environment with very little discipline. For a while, Serena enjoyed living a lavish lifestyle, not caring if she hurt anyone else in her pursuit of happiness. However, Serena has seen the error of her ways and is really trying to be a better person. She struggles every day with making the right decisions and doing her best to forget her party girl past. Serena cares deeply about her family and friends and she works very hard to help them, even when they don't think they need the help. Serena's attempts to reconcile the selfish, party girl she used to be with the responsible, mature, sweet young woman she has become is what makes her character so much fun to watch! If you answered mostly A's then chances are you like to have a good time, but you do your best to make good decisions and responsible choices every day.

Serena and Blake couldn't be more different in a lot of ways. Blake has never been a party girl. She prefers quiet nights at home with her friends and family to crazy nights out dancing. And no one would call Blake selfish. She has been working to promote charitable causes since she was younger, and she is completely selfless when it comes to helping her family and friends.

Despite their differences though, Blake does see a little of herself in Serena. They both work very hard to stand out from the crowd and they have both made the sometimes-difficult choice to fight against peer pressure. Blake strenuously avoids a lot of the traps that young stars tend to fall into — like drinking or drug use — and Serena is the same way. She has made a sincere effort to put her wild past behind her and she sticks to her guns, no matter how much her friends try to sway her. As Blake explained to *The Associated Press,* "At the heart of it all, Serena really wants to be a good person — despite all odds, despite all the chaos that's going on around her and all the other people in her life. So I think that I strive to do the right thing and not fall into the norm [like] so many young people in Hollywood who — because they were raised differently — get caught up in some of the nonsense. And I really try to steer clear of that. So, you know, we're like that in the same way. We both giggle a lot. We look alike."

Blake's character "Monica Moreland" from the film *Accepted* is the epitome of the laid-back, beautiful, all-American girl next door. She has an effortless, sweet style that her many male admirers can't get enough of. But Monica is also smart. She got into the very prestigious Harmon College, where she chose to major in media studies. Monica leads a pretty perfect life: She's gorgeous, she goes to a great school, she makes excellent grades, and has one of the cutest fraternity boys on campus as her boyfriend. But Monica isn't one to stick to the beaten path, even though it would be very easy for her to do so. In the end she dumps her boyfriend for a cooler, artsy boy, and chooses to transfer to the experimental South Harmon Institute of Technology and study photography because that is what she is most passionate about. If you answered mostly B's, then you are probably a cool, laid-back girl who isn't afraid to think for herself!

Blake and Monica have a lot in common. They both come from amazing, supportive families, they were both effortlessly cool and popular, and they both got into great colleges! And like Monica, Blake chose to follow a different path that would allow her to follow her passion, acting. It's pretty awesome that both of these ladies were willing to make difficult choices that allowed them to follow their dreams instead of just going along with the crowd!

If you answered mostly C's you are most like Bridget Vreeland

Blake's character "Bridget Vreeland" from *The Sisterhood of the Traveling Pants* is a born leader. She is strong, opinionated, and she doesn't take any attitude from anyone. She knows exactly what she wants and she always gets it, no matter how hard she has to work. She brings that same winning intensity to every area of her life, whether it's being a good friend, chasing a cute boy, or on the soccer field. Her go-getter attitude and ability to push herself to new heights of success are contagious, and she is a great influence on her sometimes more timid friends. But Bridget has a softer side, too. She knows what it's like to lose someone she loves, and she is incredibly sensitive when it comes to helping her friends through rough emotional times. Luckily, Bridget plays just as hard as she works. She is sporty, fun, and full of fantastic ideas. She is the life of every party and she really knows how to kick back and enjoy the

fruits of her labor at the end of the day. If you answered mostly C's, then you are a dynamic leader who works hard, but knows how to have fun, too.

Blake is a lot like Bridget. Blake has never been afraid to try new things, and she gives whatever she's doing one hundred percent of her effort and focus — which is probably why she's so successful! Blake knows that she has to keep working harder and pushing herself with new and challenging roles in order to grow as an actress, and she never shies away from that. Blake is also a wonderful and loyal friend, just like Bridget. She's still very close with the friends she's had since she was little, and she's always willing to drop everything if they need her.

Blake is an incredible actress and she is totally believable as each character she brings to life, but, at the end of the day, she isn't any of the girls she plays — she's just herself! Blake is a total individual, and Blake is a hard worker, but she also knows how important it is to enjoy life. She is incredibly passionate and always follows her own instincts instead of giving in to what other people expect of her. You will never find Blake following the crowd — she always stands out, in a good way! If you answered mostly D's, then you probably always stand out in a crowd, too.

Chapter 13: The Blake Basics

So you think you're Blake's biggest fan, right? You never miss *Gossip Girl*, have preordered all of the DVD's of her movies, try to match her style, and totally want a maltipoo just like hers. Well here are the Blake basics that ever fan should know!

Name: Blake Christina Lively

Birthday: August 25, 1987

Star Sign: Virgo

Hometown: Tarzana, CA

Mom: Elaine Lively

Dad: Ernie Lively

Siblings: older brothers Eric and Jason and older
     sisters Lori and Robyn

Pets: a maltipoo (a poodle and maltese mix)
     named Penny

Hair Color: Blonde

Eye Color: Blue

Height: 5'10"

Home: She splits her time between Los Angeles, CA,
     and New York, NY

High School: Burbank High School

High School Activities: cheerleading, class president,
     choir, key club

Favorite Designers: Chanel, J Brand Jeans, James Perse,
     Jimmy Choo, Marc Jacobs, Phillip Lim, Chloé

Favorite Beauty Product: Tarte lip gloss

Favorite Color: Pink

Favorite Dessert: Red velvet cupcakes, Peterbrooke's
     chocolate popcorn, chocolate anything!

Favorite Food: anything cheesy and greasy

Favorite TV: The Food Network

Favorite Actress: Angelina Jolie

Favorite Actor: Brad Pitt

Favorite Musicians: Chet Baker, Johnny Cash, the Spice Girls, and Britney Spears

Favorite Gadget: iPhone and Wii

Favorite Game: Guitar Hero

Favorite Movies: Wizard of Oz, Moulin Rouge!, and Romeo and Juliet

Favorite Vacation Spot: Hilton Waikoloa Village on the Big Island in Hawaii

Favorite Place to Get Away from It All: Johnson Mill Bed & Breakfast, Midway, Utah

Hobbies: Shopping, playing Guitar Hero, baking, creating Wii Miis of her friends

Habit She Wishes She Could Break: Always being late

Chapter 14: Blake Online

Blake Lively is on her way to being a bona fide superstar, so there is sure to be more news and information about her out there soon. Between filming new episodes of *Gossip Girl*, shooting movies, doing interviews and photo shoots, and hanging out in New York City, Blake is always on the go. So if you want to keep up with this stunning starlet, here is a list of web sites where you can get Blake updates all the time.

http://www.cwtv.com/shows/gossip-girl

This is the official *Gossip Girl* web site. It has full episodes of the show, games, a style section, pictures, quizzes, and character biographies. Check it out if you want to learn more about all things *Gossip Girl*!

http://blakelivelyweb.com/

This is an amazing fansite dedicated to Blake. They have constant news updates, pictures, videos, and a forum where you can discuss Blake with other fans.

http://sisterhoodofthetravelingpants2.warnerbros.com/

This is the official *Sisterhood of the Traveling Pants 2* website. It has widgets, downloads, information on the books and the first movie, and some special blog sections that will give you new insights into your favorite characters!

http://www.imdb.com/name/nm0515116/

This is Blake's page on the Internet Movie Database. It has tons of information about all of her roles plus all of her appearances and interviews.

Always be careful when searching online. Never give out any personal information and never arrange to meet someone in person that you've met on the web. And please keep in mind that not everything you read online is true. There are lots of people with web sites, and sometimes they make up information to make their sites more exciting. Can't find your favorite web site? Web sites come and go, so don't worry—there's sure to be another Blake site to replace it soon!